D0597030

Praise for

One Month to Live

by Kerry and Chris Shook

❝*One Month to Live* is a great way to discover the purposeful, joyful, abundant life God created you to enjoy.❞

> —RICK WARREN, senior pastor of Saddleback Church and best-selling author of *The Purpose-Driven Life*

❝Regardless of where you are on your spiritual journey, *One Month to Live* will challenge you to passionately live the life you were made for and leave an eternal legacy.❞

> —BILL HYBELS, best-selling author and senior pastor of Willow Creek Community Church

❝If you want new urgency, fresh purpose, and a sharper focus for your life, then this book is for you. Read it and your future may be changed forever!❞

> —LEE STROBEL, author of *The Case for the Real Jesus*

❝*One Month to Live* by Kerry and Chris Shook will add value to the life of every person who reads it. The questions asked and the 'Make It Count Moments' in this book will stir your soul and inspire you to begin, today, to make the rest of your life more meaningful. What Kerry and Chris present in *One Month to Live* could be life altering.❞

> —KEN BLANCHARD, author of *The One Minute Manager* and *Know Can Do!*

❝Through the ups and downs, routines and regimens of our daily existence, we can become complacent, even bored, with life. But God never meant for life to be boring. And in *One Month to Live,* Kerry and Chris Shook remind us of the true depth and meaning that God has in store for each of our lives. No matter where you are in your walk with God, this book will reveal to you a fresh and much-needed perspective. And at the end of this thirty-day journey, you will discover exactly what it means to truly live—daily . . . creatively . . . passionately!**

—ED YOUNG, senior and founding pastor of Fellowship Church and author of *Outrageous, Contagious Joy*

Too many people live with regrets, missed opportunities, and dormant dreams. You don't have to be one of them. Your life will be different if you apply the transformational principles in Kerry and Chris Shook's *One Month to Live*.

—CRAIG GROESCHEL, founding pastor of Lifechurch.tv and author of *Confessions of a Pastor*

One Month to Live
DEVOTIONAL JOURNAL

One Month to Live
DEVOTIONAL JOURNAL

Your Thirty-Day Companion
to a No-Regrets Life

by Kerry and Chris Shook
with Brian Smith

WATERBROOK
PRESS

ONE MONTH TO LIVE DEVOTIONAL JOURNAL
PUBLISHED BY WATERBROOK PRESS
12265 Oracle Boulevard, Suite 200
Colorado Springs, Colorado 80921

ISBN 978-0-30745-708-0

Produced with the assistance of The Livingstone Corporation www.livingstonecorp.com.
Project staff includes Neil Wilson and Linda Taylor. Interior design by Larry Taylor.
Typeset by Joel Bartlett, Kathleen Ristow, and Thomas Ristow.

Printed in the United States of America
2008—First Edition

10 9 8 7 6 5 4 3 2 1

SPECIAL SALES
Most WaterBrook Multnomah books are available in special quantity discounts when
purchased in bulk by corporations, organizations, and special-interest groups. Custom
imprinting or excerpting can also be done to fit special needs. For information, please
e-mail SpecialMarkets@WaterBrookMultnomah.com or call 1-800-603-7051.

Contents

Principle 1
Live Passionately

Principle 2
Love Completely

Principle 3
Learn Humbly

Principle 4
Leave Boldly

the One-Month-to-Live
Challenge

I commit with God's strength to live
the next thirty days as if they are my last
so I can experience life to the full!

_____

Your name

_____

Partner's name

Kerry & Chris Shook

Kerry and Chris Shook

*Take the one-month-to-live challenge with a friend
and log on to OneMonthToLive.com for daily
encouragement from Kerry and Chris.*

Introduction
LIVING THE DASH

LIFE
LESSON

You get to choose how to spend that little dash of time between the two dates of your earthly existence. What are you spending yours on? Are you living the dash, knowing fully who you are and why you're here? Or dashing to live, hurriedly spending precious time chasing things that really don't matter to you? The psalmist prayed, "Teach us to number our days and recognize how few they are; help us to spend them as we should" (Psalm 90:12, TLB).

Just over three thousand years ago, a 120-year-old man stood on a rocky hillside addressing a couple million homeless men, women, and children. They were the descendants of Israel, about to end a forty-year desert detour on their way to the Promised Land. His name was Moses, and he was about to die.

Moses was giving his farewell sermon. The heart of his message: "I set before you today life and prosperity, death and destruction. . . . *Now choose life . . .* that you may love the LORD your God, listen to his voice, and hold fast to him. For the LORD *is* your life" (Deuteronomy 30:15, 19-20, emphasis added).

Skip ahead a millennium or so, and we hear Jesus addressing a crowd in a similar fashion: "I have come that they may have *life*, and have it *to the full*" (John 10:10, emphasis added).

Throughout the ages, only a small percentage of people have discovered the way to live life to the fullest. These are the people who have impacted eternity. And they have looked back from their deathbeds with gratitude, not regrets.

Some of them have big names, like the apostle Paul. Well-known missionaries, evangelists, artists, and influencers from every continent line the halls of history. But some of their names few will ever know. The woman who prays for her neighborhood. The college student who volunteers at the homeless shelter. The businessperson who takes a hit for integrity's sake. The moms and dads who fill their growing kids with values like honor and respect.

These are people we may not know about now, but we'll meet them in eternity. And one day they'll meet you as well.

■ When have you lived in denial of your mortality? What were the results? How did those results differ from living intentionally aware of "the dash"? Jesus said that we find freedom in the truth (see John 8:31-32). Read Psalm 90 and consider how the author brings our short lives clearly into perspective.

■ What does this passage suggest about how we can find meaning in our few years on this earth?

If you knew you only had one month to live . . . you wouldn't hesitate to be spontaneous and risk your heart.

"As a well-spent day brings happy sleep, so life well used brings happy death."
—Leonardo da Vinci

■ What are you already doing in order to invest your time for eternity?

■ What one or two risks do you sense you need to take? More specifically, what investments of time might you need to make despite the potential embarrassment, loss, pain, or cost?

"Let us endeavor so to live that when we come to die even the undertaker will be sorry."
—Mark Twain

Why wait for a crisis—like a doctor's prognosis—to shock you into the One Month to Live mind-set? Our word crisis comes from the Greek verb *krinein*, "to decide." You can create your crisis, your point of decision, right now. Choose to see the fork in the road that confronts you every day—one path leading to mediocrity and twenty-four wasted hours, the other leading to abundant life and one more day invested for eternity.

■ What's one proactive decision you can make now that will make this day count for eternity?

A s you launch into the *One Month to Live Devotional Journal*, we're challenging you to take at least one small step of change every day for the next thirty days.

For each of those days, we've provided a few thoughts and questions to help you take the next steps in deepening your spiritual life so that you can live passionately, love completely, learn humbly, and prepare to leave boldly. If you'll commit to this journey with us, we guarantee you'll see tangible results in your everyday living. You'll be on your way to a no-regrets life.

We want you to use the journaling space to explore the ideas and process the truths discussed here.

In each day's entry you'll find a "Today's Challenge" section as well as exercises for application in the four "One Month to Live Lifestyle" collections found at the end of each section.

Like any journey, this one is most valuable and personally enriching when you share it with at least one other person. If you don't have a traveling companion, consider finding someone you trust who'll take this commitment seriously. Then plan to get together at least once a week.

Let's move ahead to Today's Challenge and claim today for eternity!

You can live with no regrets and embrace a life so abundant you'll wonder why you ever settled for less.

"To die well is the action of the whole life."
—*Richard Sibbes*

▌ Today's Challenge

Take a few minutes to talk with God about what this one-month commitment is likely to require from you. He sometimes uses unexpected timing and methods. Are you open to His plan?

Even though the journey can be unpredictable, God instructs us all to use certain standard equipment—His Word, prayer, other believers, and His Holy Spirit in our lives. Talk to God about your intention to call on these resources during the next thirty days.

Before you pray, consider reading Joshua 1:1-9, the sequel to Moses' farewell sermon.

▌ Face Time

God, thanks for promising to be present with me as I explore a more abundant life.

Every day, starting now, challenge me to take the initiative for each new step. Feed my spirit with glimpses of Your heart for me and for others. Let me experience both the rewards You've promised as I keep my eyes on You and the victory over mediocrity that You've guaranteed.

Amen.

Principle 1

Live Passionately

If you're serious about engaging in the One Month to Live lifestyle, be prepared to hang on tight. Secure any loose items. And shift your thinking from concern about security to opportunities for discovery.

You're about to leave behind the world where good enough is good enough. Where safety is more valued than significance. Where maintaining is the goal, and your secret dreams go unfulfilled. It's time to flourish. It's time to embrace your One Month to Live life!

Scary thought? You bet. We've all been burned by taking risks before.

But this time God is calling you to the center of His abundant life. His promises ensure that this risk bears rewards. With God's help, this frightening, exhilarating, satisfying adventure becomes the only true way to live.

This is the life you were made for.

Roller Coaster
RIDING THE BIG DIPPER

LIFE LESSON

The world says, "Don't be ridiculous; be reasonable. Don't stand out. Don't take risks; play it safe, and make security and comfort your primary goals in life." . . . God calls us to a life of faith, living every moment all out for Him.

Is it your goal in life to be comfortable, maintain the status quo, and avoid risk? The disciples quickly discovered the disorientation, exhaustion, terror, and exhilaration of the life-or-death risks involved in riding the roller coaster of life with Jesus. Paul, God's messenger to the Gentiles, willingly gave up everything for a ticket to ride over land and sea, in and out of jail, through sorrow and suffering—all to experience mind-boggling displays of the Holy Spirit's power.

As followers of Christ, we should come to expect risk and regard the pain and losses of life as normal, even valuable to the Christian journey. But so often our response seems to fit a different world—a fantasyland promising a nice, pain-free existence. Then, when inevitable struggles come, we think, *This can't be right. Following Jesus isn't supposed to hurt.*

Life brings pain. And sometimes following Christ actually invites suffering. But the life God offers is one of belonging and fulfillment and exciting breakthroughs. To experience it, we have to risk. Sometimes following Him will hurt . . . badly. But when we follow Jesus the promise of incredible reward is always there . . . for our reassurance and to help us endure the trials that make us stronger.

Junior high school football coaches will tell you that the players most likely to be injured are those who play tentatively.

■ *What do you see about the*
life of risky faithfulness in Jesus?
Mark 10:29-31
Luke 18:31-34
Matthew 16:21-23

in Paul?
Acts 20:16-25
Philippians 2:29-30
Philippians 3:7-14

God did not design us simply to stand by
and watch life pass as we wonder why
we aren't more fulfilled. God created us
to take risks in faith and to conquer the
giants that paralyze us with fear.

"If you wait for the perfect moment when
all is safe and assured, it may never ar-
rive. Mountains will not be climbed, races
won, or lasting happiness achieved."
—*Maurice Chevalier*

■ To change your primary goal from personal safety to adventurous obedience requires strengthening your faith. You can't become a marathon runner overnight. What's a reasonable, stretching step of faith for you to take today?

■ What might you attempt in a week or a month?

■ In what ways might God use these experiences to elevate your perspective from ground level to God level?

You may feel like you've already jumped off the roller coaster tracks and crashed on the pavement. As difficult and frightening as your life may be right now, God is still there. He cares about you beyond what you can understand or even imagine.

■ What can you do to claim God's promises of healing and comfort today?
Psalm 34:18
2 Corinthians 1:3-5
2 Corinthians 1:8-11

> *God is an expert driver. He knows right where He's going, and He's in total control when you feel afraid.*

> *"It is often said that before you die your life passes before your eyes. It is in fact true. It's called living."*
>
> —*Terry Pratchett*

■ *Why are you sometimes tempted to grab the steering wheel of your life back from God?*

■ *You might wonder, "God, are You able? Do You know how? Do You care?" What are God's answers?*

▌ Today's Challenge

Often we're tempted to play it safe and settle for far less than we were made for. I know so many people whose favorite day of the week is Someday. Countless people in every stage of life say, "Someday I'm going to go for all that life has to offer." "When I retire, then I'm going to enjoy life." "Someday I'm really going to live for God and get my act together. I'll start loving my family better." "When I make enough money, then I'm really going to spend more time with my kids." "Someday when my schedule slows down, then I'm going to get involved at church." "When I have more time, then I'll focus on being more spiritual."

Someday. One day. When. If. Then it's over. When are we going to wake up and realize *this is life?*

Write down three things that are important, though not urgent, that you have put off until "someday." Choose one and take the first steps toward accomplishing that goal today.

▌ Face Time

Father, help me find my security in You. Not in my abilities. Not in my resources. Not in my job. Not in my relationships. Not in anything I have or do . . . Nothing except You.

And in the security of You, teach me each day how to take one more step of faithful risk. I trust You to heal my hurts, past, present, and future. Help me to live each day without any regrets.

Time Squared

SPENDING YOUR MOST VALUABLE RESOURCE

LIFE LESSON

Time once spent cannot be reclaimed. Once an hour, minute, or moment is over, it's gone forever. However, we can redeem the remaining time we have. We can reconsider our God-given purpose and the eternal legacy we want to leave behind and allow them to guide our schedule moving forward.

Picture your life as a village with three buildings—a school, a bank, and your home.

The school is your past, where you go to study the curriculum of your prior experiences. But you can't change the bad or relive the good. You don't live there.

The bank is your future. You visit it to plan your investment of today's time and resources. But you don't live there either. You can only prepare for the future.

Trying to live in the past or the future means vacating your home—the here and now. For a life of purpose, you must live in the present, where you can make a difference by applying past lessons and making wise choices to impact the future.

> *"He who neglects the present moment throws away all he has."*
> —Johann Friedrich von Schiller

■ Where have you been living recently? Describe your relationship with your past, present, and future.

■ What, practically, might you do to live more in the present, while applying lessons from your past and investing in your future?

■ Identify God's priorities as revealed in the following passages. Watch for words like better, rather, and most important. Write out a list of God's priorities.
Psalm 63:3
Proverbs 16:16
Proverbs 17:1
Ezekiel 18:23
Mark 12:29-31
Acts 5:29

■ What's one way you could take time from lower priorities and devote it to a higher priority? Be specific.

It almost seems like a natural law of physics. When we increase our energy and level of engagement, we multiply our time. . . . I'm not talking about how to add years to your life but rather how to add life to your years.

"Tell me to what you pay attention, and I will tell you who you are."
—José Ortega y Gasset

Charging or discharging? Say you spend an hour with a friend or loved one. You can keep your heart closed off, or you can open up and engage personally. Either choice costs sixty minutes. But one sucks the energy out of the time, out of you; the other saturates the minutes with life.

■ *Brainstorm ways to improve your energy management for one top priority, not by necessarily devoting additional time, but by engaging more personally and deeply.*

■ *Think of one tangible thing you can do today and write it down.*

There is great freedom in learning to operate with an eternal perspective and not just by the watch on our wrist. A regular time of rest and recovery, a sabbath, is essential. . . .We must be willing to live by an eternal clock, listening to God in our lives as well as listening to our bodies and hearts.

■ *Are you yielding to your divine design and taking a weekly sabbath? What is one new way you might honor your built-in need for rest?*

"A man's heart has only enough life in it to pursue one object fully."
—*Charles Haddon Spurgeon*

▌ Today's Challenge

Collect Scripture passages—as many as you can—that clarify God's priority system. Use a concordance or a Bible search program on your computer to find words like *better, rather, greater, important,* and *more precious*. To get started, have a look at Psalm 37:16-17; Proverbs 8:10-11; Daniel 3:28; Matthew 23:23; and 1 Peter 1:6-7.

As you reassign your time and energy for maximum life and eternal impact, make a habit of consulting the Bible about God's priorities.

▌ Face Time

God, I've been killing time. I've wasted so many chances to do important things for You.

I'm sorry.

Take my priorities—the ones I really own, down deep—and show me how to make them more like Your priorities. Make my heart beat faster for the things that excite You. Most of all, give me a heart that can never get enough time with You.

Power Surge
CONNECTING WITH THE ULTIMATE SOURCE

LIFE LESSON

We have to be connected to a power source beyond ourselves—a power source that never wavers, flickers, or leaves us in the dark. We have to move from willpower to the real power that comes from a connection to our Creator.

We need the power to change. The problem is, we often think we can make the necessary changes with a little willpower, and we don't see how dependent we are on God's power.

■ *Think about some specific ways you can adjust your thinking and your actions to rely more on God when you are*
- *confused and frightened (Psalm 46:10-11)*
- *feeling stupid or unimportant (1 Corinthians 1:26-31)*
- *exhausted (Isaiah 40:28-31)*
- *defeated by circumstances (2 Corinthians 12:7-10)*
- *feeling incompetent (2 Corinthians 3:5)*
- *struggling hard for results (Colossians 1:29)*
- *feeling totally self-sufficient (1 Corinthians 10:12)*

*The key to spiritual heath is maintaining
a strong relationship with your Creator.
If you are connected to your Creator, you
will grow like you've never grown before,
and you'll experience real power to make
lasting changes.*

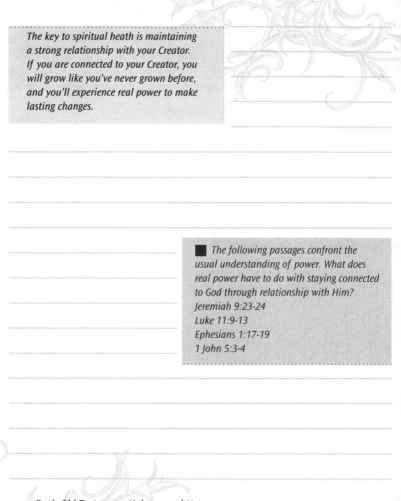

■ *The following passages confront the
usual understanding of power. What does
real power have to do with staying connected
to God through relationship with Him?*
Jeremiah 9:23-24
Luke 11:9-13
Ephesians 1:17-19
1 John 5:3-4

Both Old Testament Hebrew and New
Testament Greek have multiple words
that can be translated "know." Both
the Hebrew *yada* (as in Jeremiah 9:24)
and the Greek *ginosko* (as in Ephesians
1:17) often imply intimate, personal,
experiential knowledge—not just factual
knowledge.

■ *Staying connected with Jesus means* **constant communication** *(see 1 Thessalonians 5:17-18). In a typical day, what's one specific time you could include greater conversation with your Friend and Lord?*

■ *Use these scriptures to find out how communication with Jesus will give you power today and write down what you discover.*
Matthew 26:41
Philippians 4:6-7
2 Thessalonians 1:11-12
1 Peter 5:7

Communication and confession . . . the key for moving from willpower to real power.

■ *Staying connected also means* **constant confession**. *Why does agreeing with Jesus about your mistakes and sins give you freedom and power?*
Psalm 32
1 John 1:7-9

■ *Brainstorm one simple way you can remember to confess your sins throughout your day.*

"The first purpose of prayer is to know God."

—*Charles L. Allen*

*I*f you forget everything else from this thirty-day journey, we hope you will remember and practice one thing . . .

Stay connected with Jesus!

That's how you switch from willpower to God's real power!

This is the heartbeat of the abundant life. During the rest of this month's journey, many topics will help you understand better how to stay connected with Jesus. And some teachings will be impossible to put into practice *without* staying connected.

Remember who you are: you're a branch; He's the Vine.

You stay connected, and *He* will produce results in your life.

▌ Today's Challenge

Write down a simple plan to become better connected with Jesus. What are your next steps toward sustaining constant communication and confession each day? Your plan might involve a partner, sticky notes, watch alarm, cell phone, or note cards around the house. Maybe you'll remember to connect with Him every time you walk through a doorway, sit down, use your turn signal, or finish a conversation.

Keep your plan simple and focus on what works for you as a continual reminder. If that idea doesn't work or becomes ineffective after a while, pick up another method. Change the plan according to how well it keeps you connected.

Once you've written down your plan and put it into practice, you'll be amazed at how a little intentional effort to connect with Jesus can make all the difference in your day.

▌ Face Time

God, I need Your help to stop relying on my own power instead of Yours. Especially when it comes to

But Your wisdom is endless. Your abilities are boundless. And You care more about me than I can ever know. So I want to live in Your power today.

You know what's on my heart right now, so I'm asking for Your help with . . .

I know that trying to live in my own strength is wrong. Thank You for always forgiving me. Help me live Your way today.

Oxygen Mask
BREATHING FIRST

LIFE LESSON

If you're going to make the most of your time on earth, living a no-regrets lifestyle, then you need to engage fully with those around you. . . . The only way to accomplish these goals of authentic living is first to take time and focus on yourself. If you're not healthy spiritually, physically, emotionally, and relationally, how can you move beyond yourself and invest in others?

In the apostle John's account of the Last Supper, he started out with an unexpected editorial comment: "Jesus knew that the Father had put all things under his power, and that he had come from God and was returning to God" (John 13:3). In other words, Jesus had made a priority of maintaining His spiritual and emotional health: He knew exactly who He was, and He had a strong, intimate connection with His Father.

Why is this fact important in John 13? Because this knowledge gave Jesus the strength of character to serve His men: "So he got up from the meal, took off his outer clothing, and wrapped a towel around his waist. After that, he poured water into a basin and began to wash his disciples' feet" (verses 4-5).

As we've seen, Jesus believed that appropriate self-care is a prerequisite to loving and caring for others (see Matthew 22:37-39). So today we're going to focus on our physical and emotional health.

> "Nobody holds a good opinion of a man who has a low opinion of himself."
> —Anthony Trollope

You have to first take time to get healthy so you can impact the world around you.

■ What are some of the differences between legitimate self-care and selfishness?
Romans 12:3
Ephesians 5:28-29
1 Timothy 4:12, 16

How you treat your body has a direct and lasting impact on the quality of life you enjoy.

■ Rewrite in your own words what Psalm 139:13-16 says about your body.

■ What are a few new ways you want to "honor God with your body," which belongs to Him (1 Corinthians 6:19-20)? Choose a better diet? Get more rest or exercise? See a doctor? Work toward a healthier body concept? Be specific.

■ In what ways will your spiritual health— your staying connected with God—impact your physical health?

We may not be able to control what we feel, but we definitely can control what we do with those emotions—how they affect our thoughts and behavior.

■ How do each of these passages demonstrate both honesty
Matthew 26:36-39; Psalm 73

. . . and self-control?
Psalm 43; Ephesians 4:22-27

■ Do your emotions ever get out of control and cause problems for you and/or others? Brainstorm some possible action steps toward self-control, steps that will still allow you to acknowledge and express your feelings.

■ Do you sometimes put your emotions on hold and not allow yourself to express them? If so, brainstorm some action steps you could take toward being more emotionally honest, yet still controlling your actions.

■ How do you see your spiritual health impacting your emotional health? In what ways does spiritual health impact emotional health?
Galatians 5:16-25
Romans 6:6-14

"Never apologize for showing feeling. When you do so, you apologize for the truth."
—Benjamin Disraeli

▶ Today's Challenge

Look back over your journaling from today and choose one goal for your physical health and one for your emotional health. Or you might renew your commitment to goals you're already working toward.

Choose goals that are stretching but realistic. And make them measurable.

If you drop the ball, pick it back up. Remember, you can adjust your goal any time you need to.

Start now!

▶ Face Time

Father, You made me and You bought me. I'm Yours twice over. Because You love me so much, I want to be healthy for You. And for all the people You want me to love.

Help me remember to stay constantly connected with You while I . . .
[describe your physical and emotional health goals].

Monkey Bars
RISKING GREATNESS

LIFE LESSON

The only way to risk greatness is to trust God with all areas of your life. . . . He wants us to trust Him to accomplish incredible things we could never achieve on our own.

One normal morning, an abnormal thing happened to Simon Peter. He and his fishing compadres were cleaning up after a fruitless night on Lake Galilee, when Jesus the carpenter told them to launch back out. He then guided them to a record-breaking haul.

Peter fell before the Master and begged, "Go away from me, Lord; I am a sinful man!" He may also have been thinking, *And unworthy and incapable of being with a world-changer like You.* Peter was filled with terror, because he was convinced that a minnow-grubber could play no role in God's eternal plan.

Jesus knew otherwise. "Don't be afraid," He said. "From now on you'll catch men" (see Luke 5:1-11).

That day, Jesus revealed the unexpected potential in Peter's life. Changed from fisher-man to man-fisher, Peter was destined to become the rock-solid follower on which Jesus built His church.

The only way to risk greatness is to trust God with all areas of your life. Not only is it exhausting to hang onto the monkey bars so tightly, but it keeps us from pursuing the much larger and more fulfilling dreams God has for us.

■ *Imagine you were guaranteed pain-free success. Describe five great accomplishments you would love to pursue for God.*

Each and every day I have to come to the place where I realize I can't control everything in my life, and I have to let go and surrender to God. He always catches me, and that's when I feel His peace and strength in the stressful moments of life.

■ *Take a moment to think about what past disappointments may have conditioned you not to trust God to catch you. This is a multifaceted question, but write your initial thoughts here.*

■ What do the following passages promise? What don't they promise?
John 10:27-30
Romans 8:31-39
2 Timothy 4:16-18

■ Summarize in your own words, in your own way, the kind of success and protection God guarantees.

"They tell about a fifteen-year-old boy in an orphans' home who had an incurable stutter. One Sunday the minister was detained and the boy volunteered to say the prayer in his stead. He did it perfectly, too, without a single stutter. Later he explained, 'I don't stutter when I talk to God. He loves me.'"

—Bennett Cerf

■ Consider the statement, "To know God is to trust Him." Do you agree? Why or why not? (See 2 Timothy 1:12; Ephesians 3:16-21.)

■ Why does our constant connection with Jesus make faith-filled risks worth taking?
John 14:12-14
Deuteronomy 31:8
Matthew 28:18-20

If we knew our days were numbered . . . we wouldn't be worried about what others think of us or what they would say. We wouldn't be worried about failing or wasting time, because we would recognize that regret would outweigh either of them.

▶ Today's Challenge

What's one risk you want to take for God? Write a list of pros and cons. What are the worst and best possible end scenarios?

Now ask God to help you see the cons in their proper perspective; that is, in relation to His greatness and love.

Next, ask God to fill you with His strength, courage, and creativity to reach the goal.

What will be your first step toward taking this risk for God?

▶ Face Time

Okay, God, we both know what I've been putting off. And we both know why. I'm putting this situation in Your hands:

The whats and the whys can change. But You never change. Your power and authority in my life are absolute. I want to take this risk. Walk through it with me, please.

Thank You for Your power that enables me to do Your will, focusing my attention on this moment so that I can live without regrets.

Dreamsicle
THAWING OUT YOUR FROZEN DREAMS

LIFE LESSON

God has put us here for a reason and planted dreams within us so we can do our part in seeing them realized.

"If a man wants his dreams to come true, he must wake up."

—Anonymous

■ Look below at the apostle Paul's enthusiasm for his God-given dream. What would you be saying if you felt this same way about God's dream for you? (If you don't know God's dream for you, try putting possible dreams into words like Paul's. Say them out loud, and see how they sound to you.)
- "I am so eager to preach the gospel" (Romans 1:15).
- "Woe to me if I do not preach the gospel!" (1 Corinthians 9:16).
- "One thing I do: Forgetting what is behind and straining toward what is ahead, I press on toward the goal to win the prize for which God has called me" (Philippians 3:13-14).

■ What does God want you to do about dreams from Him that you once pursued, but have abandoned? (See Revelation 2:4-5.)

■ Some people's "doubt" is a smoke screen for resistance to God. But what is God's attitude toward a genuine doubter? (See Jude 1:22.) Why?

■ When you doubt your ability to fulfill a God-given dream—to achieve something He wants for you—what does God say about His willingness and ability to fulfill that dream? (See 1 John 5:14-15; Jeremiah 32:17.)

There is one who exists for no other reason than to play games and deceive you. This enemy fears your heart, because he knows what God can do through ordinary people like you to make an extraordinary difference in the world.

"Our doubts are traitors, and make us lose the good we often might win, by fearing to attempt."
—William Shakespeare

■ Satan's doubt-inspiring voice can sound very much like the voice of reason, even the voice of righteousness (2 Corinthians 11:13-15). What will you do to obey God's command and claim His promise in 1 Peter 5:8-11?

■ When Satan whispers, "You're not up to it," why is this message so convincing? Why is it dangerous?

"No one is a firmer believer in the power of prayer than the devil; not that he practices it, but he suffers from it."
—Guy H. King

God delights in healing our wounds and turning them into strengths to accomplish the dreams He has for us.

■ *Do you need God's healing? What will you do to claim His promises right now? (See Psalm 147:3 and Isaiah 61:1-3, a promise of the Messiah's ministry to us.)*

▶ Today's Challenge

Choose a frozen dream that you think God wants you to pursue. If your faith is still weak and your wounds are still deep, He understands if you start with something small.

Live in dreamland for at least a few minutes. Imagine the end picture if this dream is fulfilled. Describe the steps it would take to fulfill this dream.

Now you have your prayer list for the real world—the one God's in charge of. Pray and ask God to fill you with enthusiastic confidence in Him and His dream for you.

Write a tentative date for your first step and share it with someone.

▶ Face Time

My frozen dream is in Your hands, Lord. Help me to trust You to let it thaw out. I choose to believe that, if it's Your dream for me, You'll give me hope, passion, and power to fulfill it. And if it's not, please give me new direction.

Please heal me of [describe your disappointment wounds] _____

_____

And give me strength to resist Satan's lies. In particular, I'm wrestling with [share your

doubts] _____.

Thank You for Your promises to me. Help me to trust You more.

kick Start
LIVING LIFE FULL THROTTLE

LIFE
LESSON

God's power is available to help us live the lives for which He created us, but so much of the time we live in our own strength. We try to climb the hills and tackle problems without adequate power to finish the course.

Ever feel powerless? That's good! In ourselves, we *are* lacking real power for abundant living.

God purposely designed us with weaknesses, so that we'd depend on Him for complete, all-out living. The apostle Paul tells us that God chose the foolish and the weak and the lowborn to accomplish His great plan (1 Corinthians 1:25–2:5). Paul learned to boast in his weaknesses, because they allowed God to prove Himself strong (2 Corinthians 12:7-10).

Trusting God is often uncomfortable, because our faith in Him is a lifelong work in progress. But He's patient with us, as long as we remain willing to take the next uncomfortable step. Whether we believe it or not, this often awkward process is the means by which God causes us to accomplish the miraculous.

A critical transformation takes place when we realize we have all God's power available to us.

■ What will it look like and feel like when you voluntarily choose to live with God in humble dependence on Him?
Isaiah 66:1-2
Micah 6:8
Matthew 18:1-4
James 4:6-10

The greatest power we need in our lives is the power to begin again.

■ Describe one "crash" you have experienced in life—a major relationship explosion or disappointment—that you feared you'd never recover from.

■ What did Paul teach about God's power to help us begin again? Answer in terms of your own situation.
1 Timothy 1:12-17
Ephesians 2:1-9
Romans 4:4-8

Jesus looks with compassion right into your heart. He sees the guilt and . . . the shame. But He says that because of the power of His love for you, failure is never final.

"So what do we do? Anything. Something. So long as we just don't sit there. If we screw it up, start over. Try something else. If we wait until we've satisfied all the uncertainties, it may be too late."

—Lee Iacocca

■ *Read Psalm 103:1-18 and then humbly admit to God the sins and failures that are on your heart. Verbally release your guilt to God in response to His promise of forgiveness.*

■ *The one step remaining is the turnaround power play. You need to surrender to God's strength—that is, deny yourself (Luke 9:23), give yourself over to God's way of doing things. Why is God's way better than your way?*
Deuteronomy 8:5-6
Deuteronomy 30:15-16
Proverbs 3:5-8
Proverbs 14:12
Isaiah 55:6-9

In Ephesians, Paul says, "I pray that you will begin to understand how incredibly great his power is to help those who believe him. It is that same mighty power that raised Christ from the dead" (1:19-20, TLB). He'll give you all the power you need for the One Month to Live lifestyle.

■ *Take a few minutes to surrender your willpower to God's power.*

▌ **Today's Challenge**

We've all experienced crashes in life—times when we tried and failed. Often, our response is to give up and move on. The memory of the experience is painful, so we choose to forget.

Your challenge today is to mentally revisit that disappointment. Did you fail to prepare adequately? Give up too easily? Prayerfully consider trying again, this time relying on God's power and provision.

▌ **Face Time**

I'd like to begin again. But I don't have the power. So, God of second chances, I'm completely dependent on You.

And I'm not even completely sure of the way. My way failed. So guide me in Your way. Starting now.

I need You to resurrect my confidence in a worthwhile future. Please work in my heart with the power that raised Jesus from the dead (Ephesians 1:19-20).

Passion Quotient Checklist

❑ I'm willing to take risks in order to obey God and make the most of this life, even when I'm afraid.

❑ I know (most of the time) that God is better at steering my life than I am.

❑ My friends would say I'm usually present in the present.

❑ I understand God's highest priorities, and I'm making progress toward making them more my own.

❑ I can identify at least one time I recently depended on God's power.

❑ I often remember to use communication and confession to connect me to Christ.

❑ I'm responsible with my physical health, and I have a positive body concept.

❑ I'm emotionally honest, but I don't let my feelings drive me.

❑ I trust God to catch me when I take a risk for Him.

❑ I'm excited about pursuing my God-given dreams.

❑ God has made progress in healing my emotional wounds.

❑ Recently, in God's power, I've managed to get up and try again after a failure.

❑ I'm getting better at surrendering to God's way of doing things.

❑ I may not be living at full throttle, but my friends would say I'm accelerating.

Now evaluate other areas for focused development in your life—the ones you think God is prompting you to pursue in the coming months. Look back over Days 2 through 8 and choose applications from one or two of your One Month to Live Lifestyle exercises that you'd like to build into your life. Write them under "Principle 1" in "My Maximum Life Plan" on page 162. If you aren't already in the habit of staying connected with Jesus, be sure to include goals from Day 4.

One Month to Live Lifestyle
Passionate Ways to Live

The ways to cultivate passion are countless and varied. The "One Month to Live Lifestyle" offers fresh ideas for putting the Week 1 principles into practice. Browse around, and if something stands out and seems like "you," then run with it.

Passion Passages

Risk and Trust
Psalm 119:60
Psalm 147:1-3
Romans 8:28
Philippians 1:12-14

Priorities
Ecclesiastes 7:1-8
Hosea 6:6
Luke 18:9-14
Acts 4:19-20
Romans 12:3
1 Timothy 4:8

Drawing on God's Power
Psalm 51
Psalm 111
Zechariah 4:6
1 Corinthians 1:17-21
2 Corinthians 4:7
Philippians 4:19

Self-Care
Exodus 20:8-11
Mark 6:30-32
John 11:20-44
Galatians 6:1-5
Philippians 2:3-11

Quick Takes

Applications requiring just a few minutes.

For practice, break out of an inconsequential rut: rearrange your work space; have eggs for dinner; take the scenic route to work.

◆ Choose a simple "someday" task that you've been putting off and schedule it on your calendar.

◆ Do a chore, remembering and enjoying God's presence every moment. You might sing to Him.

◆ Take a break.

◆ Stop and ask God for His power to do everything you encounter during the next hour.

◆ Tell God about one worry or one happy thought that's on your mind.

◆ Be honest with God about one recent mess-up. Accept His forgiveness and ask for His power to help you overcome that temptation in the next twenty-four hours.

◆ Consider the way God made you, your personality and experiences, and write a list of ten aspects of your inner self that show God's loving craftsmanship. (Tape the list to your mirror.)

◆ Call someone you trust—someone appropriate for this conversation—to talk about a feeling you've been suppressing. Ask that person to pray for the Holy Spirit's help in dealing with that emotion.

◆ Give someone else control of a small decision you usually like to make.

◆ Perform an act of service that involves the risk of a bruise, dirty hands, or mild embarrassment. Take a potted plant or cookies to a neighbor. Invite a friend to pray with you over a local school or business.

◆ Create a mind map of your past and present life dreams. Write *DREAMS* in the middle of a page, and use words or drawings to thaw out and record as many of your dreams as possible.

◆ Prepare a meal you've always wanted to try, but never have. For extra credit, invite some friends over to try it with you.

◆ Think of one pursuit you're avoiding because you fear failure. Think, talk, or write about the worst that can happen if you tried it and failed. What would you do if that worst case actually happened?

Risking Greatness
Exodus 3:1-12
Numbers 14:1-30
Joshua 1:5-9
Matthew 10:16-20
Hebrews 13:5-6

Courage to Follow Your Dreams
Luke 22:31-32
Galatians 6:7-10
Hebrews 10:19-24
Revelation 3:14-16

Beginning Again
Psalm 119:1-6
Proverbs 11:2
Proverbs 16:18-19
Proverbs 18:12
Lamentation 3:40
Matthew 16:24-28

Day Jobs

Applications that take an hour or so.

Connecting Metaphors

Jesus and His disciples grew up around vineyards, so He chose the word picture of the vine and the branches recorded in John 15 to help them understand the need to be connected with Him.

What if Jesus were here in the flesh today, sharing the same truth with people in our culture—with office workers, truckers, teachers, factory workers, salespeople, business executives, students, or athletes?

Express your own metaphor to illustrate our life-giving and fruit-producing connection with Christ.

Once you've developed your metaphor, share it with someone else.

Time-Investment Pointer:

Minutes stack up to become hours. Don't minimize the loss of a minute wasted. Or the value of a minute invested.

Self-Care Spa

Spend an hour or two caring for yourself—and do something you don't often do. Go for a nature walk, jog, work out, or join a pickup basketball game at the park. Write a letter to God or someone else about your fear, pain, anger, depression, or another strong emotion. (Take at least a day before deciding whether to send the letter.) Allow yourself a holy indulgence.

Doubtful Dream Diagnosis

Talk to a friend about a God-given dream that you doubt. Unpack the obstacles that hold you back—pain from the past, reliance on self, impatience. Think of one step you will take to help overcome one obstacle, then do it!

Begin-Again Coach

Meet with someone who, by God's power, has successfully gotten back on the bike after a crash. Ask that person about the feelings, thoughts, and actions at each stage of the process. (Alternatives: Read a book, listen to a podcast, or watch a DVD about such a person.) Write down at least two practical ideas you want to apply to your own second-chance project—and give 'em a try.

Time Release

Applications to be completed over days or weeks.

Life Inventory and Cost/Benefit Analysis

If you haven't done so already, complete Exercise 1 in the Day 3 "Make It Last for Life" section (page 22 of *One Month to Live*). Consider asking others—family, co-workers, friends—to help track your use of time.

Design a time journal that best fits your personal style. Ideas include:

◆ A diary, even one as simple as a pocket notepad

◆ A chart divided into intervals of an hour, fifteen minutes, or whatever degree of detail you want

◆ A wall calendar on which you use symbols to depict and record your use of time

◆ A row of labeled containers into which you place, say, a penny or a jelly bean for every half-hour interval devoted to each type of activity

Practice Makes Permanent

Some have suggested it takes only twenty-one days to form a habit. Choose a habit you'd like to cultivate or strengthen. Then establish a daily plan for the next week or more.

Here are a few habits you might consider developing:

◆ Spend fifteen minutes in prayer each day.

◆ Invest fifteen minutes in Bible reading each day.

◆ Spend thirty minutes of quality time with your spouse or another family member.

◆ Exercise at least three days a week.

◆ Eat at least one healthy meal each day.

◆ Take one small risk of obedience each day.

◆ Somehow remind yourself three times a day to give back to God something that belongs in His hands, not yours.

The Possible Dream

Choose a dream you could get excited about, if only you could believe it were possible. You might choose to tackle a five-day dream or to begin working on a five-year dream. Pray about it and talk with friends or family members—but only those who will cheer you on.

Establish a plan that lays out measured daily or weekly steps toward the ultimate goal. (Prayerful planning for a huge dream might take several days in itself.) Then implement your plan, drawing on God's strength, as well as human accountability and support along the way.

"What we love to do we find time to do."
—John Lancaster Spalding

Principle 2

Love Completely

You've heard it before: "It's all about relationships."

But **what** exactly does this refer to? Everything! You name it.
Everything in life comes down to how we relate to people,
how we relate to God, or how we relate to ourselves.

The power of relationships is the driving force behind
all of God's creation. He created us in His image to love
and to keep company with us.

He invented friendships and marriage and families
and organizations all built around relationships.

The heartbeat of every story ever told, written, sung, or performed
is relationships. Why? Because we all have a driving interest
in how our minds and hearts interact with others.

This week we dive deeply into this most fundamental and
universal of all themes, working toward a new level of
expertise in connections of the heart.

Heart of the Matter
RELATING AND NOT WAITING

LIFE
LESSON

When all is said and done, relationships are all that really matter. It doesn't matter how much money we have, where we live, or how many beautiful toys we've collected. None of these can comfort us, console us, cry with us, or love us. Our investment in the people we care about is the only legacy that has the power to endure beyond our lifetime.

All of us are designed as relational beings, social creatures who yearn to belong. It's the way God made us—in His image.

■ Are you generally comfortable being alone? What happens to you when you're isolated for a long time? What might those who know you say happens to you when you've been alone for a long time?

■ What are some reasons you need other people in your life?

We're designed for social and emotional intimacy with those around us, but our desires are polluted by our selfish inclination to make it all about us.

■ Describe a few sins of others that have had a negative effect in your relationships.

■ Now describe some of your own relationship-damaging sins.

■ What would you like your attitude toward sin—both yours and theirs—to be?
Proverbs 8:12-13
Romans 12:9-10

■ *Everyone desperately needs God's love. In your own words, describe the way God's love for you provides you with love for others. The following passages from 1 John may help:*
3:16
4:7-12
4:16
4:19

Love can't be bought, but it definitely carries a price, and it's called sacrifice. Love always means risking pain. . . . Pain is an inherent part of any significant relationship.

"*Love is life. All, everything that I understand, I understand only because I love. Everything is, everything exists, only because I love.*"

—Leo Tolstoy

Your problem is not that you don't love God enough. It's that you don't understand how much He loves you. If you could grasp just a little bit of how much God loves you, you'd surrender all areas of your life to Him.

*G*od paid a high price to have an eternal relationship with you—the sacrifice of Jesus. As you grow in your understanding of the depth of love God showed you in giving His Son to pay for your sins, your *experience* of His love will grow as well. That is, your sense of understanding, of belonging, of acceptance and security, of confidence, of optimism, will continue to grow, and you'll experience many other benefits as well.

Those feelings are a gift you will come to pass along to other people, having received it first yourself.

How are you experiencing God's amazing love?

▶ Today's Challenge

If you've never experienced the fullness of God's love for you, it's time you did. The life He offers you, paid for by Jesus' death, is found simply by asking for it. The specific words aren't important, but here's a prayer you might say:

> God, I think the reason I haven't felt Your love is because I haven't been fully aware of it. Help me to finally see it now. Thank You, Jesus, for dying to end the influence of evil on my life. Thank You for loving me despite all You know about me. Thank You for accepting me without reserve or qualifications. Live in me today and change me.

Growing in your understanding of God's love for you is a journey best shared with someone else who knows both you and Jesus well. Share your decision with someone close to you so that person can challenge, pray for, and encourage you.

▶ Face Time

Lord, You know which people are the most important in my life. Sometimes they're also the hardest part of my life. And I don't always know what to do, how best to respond, or what results my actions will have on them.

But more important than any relational advice or techniques is Your love. Open my eyes and my heart to understand and experience Your bottomless, endless love. And change me simply by being there.

Ocean

EXPLORING THE DEPTHS OF FORGIVENESS

> **LIFE LESSON**
>
> *Our sins, faults, and failures don't go away—we either confess or suppress. . . . The key to how we leave this earth basically comes down to how we experience forgiveness and extend it to those around us.*

The ocean is a great metaphor for illustrating the boundless depths of God's forgiveness. But the deep sea also teaches another lesson about forgiveness.

If you studied the hydrosphere—that is, the water system for the whole world—you'd discover that all water sources—lakes, rivers, ponds, your bath water—are ultimately supplied by the ocean. The sun evaporates ocean water, which rises and drifts over land as clouds. The clouds drop rain, which accumulates in creeks, rivers, and lakes. So the H_2O that flows from those freshwater sources to your faucet is ultimately provided by the ocean.

Forgiveness flows in the same kind of cycle. Whenever you or anyone else offers forgiveness, the source of that forgiveness is God. Even those people who have not accepted His forgiveness are revealing His image in them when they forgive others. But especially for those who know Jesus, the transformed heart is increasingly becoming like the forgiving heart of God.

> *"Tis the most tender part of love, each other to forgive."*
> —John Sheffield

■ Many Jesus-followers have times when they doubt that God's forgiveness is deep enough to cover everything, forever. In your own words, write a letter to yourself from God, based on the truth found in these passages:
Ephesians 1:7-8
Hebrews 4:14-16
Hebrews 8:12
1 John 5:11-15

■ How completely do you accept God's forgiveness? Do you usually believe it's real, or do you live in persistent skepticism?

■ When someone forgives you, do you feel relief? Or do you keep beating yourself up?

■ How does your ability to accept forgiveness influence your willingness to extend forgiveness to others?

If you try to live without forgiving, you won't survive. It is essential that we forgive for our own sakes; otherwise we'll drown in bitterness.

"Anger makes you smaller, while forgiveness forces you to grow beyond what you were."
—Cherie Carter-Scott

■ Read the story of the prostitute and the Pharisee in Luke 7:36-50. Simon the Pharisee gave some of the "logical" reasons not to forgive the woman. What are some reasons you have trouble forgiving people around you?

■ What did Jesus say in response to those reasons and to justify forgiving the prostitute?

■ What do you think Jesus would say about your reasons for withholding forgiveness?

When I reveal my heart to God, the healing starts. I breathe out the bitterness, and then I can breathe in forgiveness.

■ Anger—even toward God—is a natural emotion. But harbored anger becomes self-damaging bitterness (Ephesians 4:26-27). Are you angry with God? He wants you to be honest with Him. Write a prayer to God based on Psalm 73:21-26.

■ *Are you angry with anyone? Tell God exactly how you feel. Take all the time you need.*

■ *Then read Ephesians 4:32–5:2. Turn to God and ask His forgiveness for anything you've done wrong. Then ask Him for the power, as His child, to imitate Him and forgive others just as He has forgiven you.*

We can't give what we haven't received. We know we've received forgiveness, but we don't really understand the depth of God's mercy, which makes it that much harder for us to forgive others. If I can understand a little bit of how much Christ has forgiven me, it's a whole lot easier to forgive others who've hurt me.

▶ Today's Challenge

Do you consistently drop your sins into the infinite depths of God's forgiveness, or do you still need to develop this habit?

Read Hebrews 10:10-24. Notice how the words *one* and *all* are used over and over.

Spend a few minutes talking to God about anything that's bothering your conscience.

Finally, ask God to use your new freedom to help you forgive anyone who's offended you. Tell Him how you want your new attitude to change your thinking and actions toward that person.

▶ Face Time

Thank You so much for the amazing freedom I find in the depths of Your forgiveness.

Sometimes I refuse Your forgiveness. Help me remember how much You always want me back.

Please keep me so aware of Your love that it becomes more natural for me to forgive others.

Everest

SCALING THE OBSTACLES TO UNITY

LIFE LESSON

If we were counting the days before we left this earth, we would be looking for ways to build bridges, to bring about healing, and to enjoy our most important relationships. No one wants to leave this earth with unfinished business. We want to leave our loved ones having experienced the summit of our relationships as the result of our courage to love.

We all have relational mountains to climb. And they're all challenging. Being able to work in teams to overcome our relational obstacles is one of the most important skills in life.

Consider some of your most important relationships—marriage, parents, children, siblings, church, friendships, workplace. All of them will involve problems at times, but they also provide opportunities to grow and bring greater fulfillment through deeper intimacy.

Often, you'll find that you're the one who needs to take the initiative to get others thinking together. If you wait for other people to make the first move, you'll only grow in passive resentment. By acknowledging and then solving relational problems, we affirm that our relationships are too important to let them suffer or stagnate. Helping others partner with you in seeking healthy patterns of relating is what today's lesson is all about.

> *"Coming together is a beginning. Keeping to-gether is progress. Working together is success."*
> —Henry Ford

Rather than cling to the ideal—that this spouse, friend, business partner, or team was the right fit and you'd always understand each other—you must realize that differences of opinion are natural and inevitable parts of every relationship.

■ Which of the relational mountains—misunderstandings, a "me first" attitude, mistakes, or something else—tends to come between you and others? Describe one recurring situation.

■ Come up with a practical plan for successfully scaling the peak in the situation you just described. Consider how to anticipate it, what to tell yourself as you're dealing with the obstacle, what to say to the other person and what not to do or say. Consider this wisdom from Proverbs:
12:6
15:1
17:27-28
18:13, 17

We have to learn how to compromise and discover creative solutions that meet the needs of both people. If we truly love someone, it will be easier to change our agenda by having an open dialogue.

■ *Our ability to accept and understand others grows as we develop new thought habits about people. Use the apostle Paul's instructions found in the passages below to come up with your own one-sentence messages that you can habitually play in your mind.*
Colossians 3:12-15
Romans 15:1-3
1 Thessalonians 5:14
Galatians 6:1-2

To accept others means that we stop trying to change them and we start trying to understand them.

■ *Read these passages, then come up with a few direct ways you might actively love specific people around you. Even small gestures of compassion count.*
Proverbs 25:21-22
Matthew 5:43-47
Luke 6:38
Galatians 6:7-10

■ *As your consistent love helps others grow in security, how will both you and they benefit? Be specific.*

It's not easy—relationships aren't for wimps. And it's going to take some supernatural help: God's power to love. But the supply is limitless, and the price of His resources never goes up, because they're free.

▶ Today's Challenge

Describe a typical conflict in your life. Prayerfully write out the general script, including the way the conflict starts, escalates, and ultimately ends. Think about how you want to change the pattern, and then think through how you'd like to revise the situation to work toward resolution. If possible, consider sharing your scenario with a trusted friend or your spouse.

When you're finished, take a few moments to pray. Ask God to help you as you work to improve the relationship.

▶ Face Time

Lord, thank You for being my Friend and for showing me how great it feels to be loved and accepted. I want to help other people feel that same way. I want them to be safe in their friendship with me, to trust me the way I'm learning to trust You.

Help me let go of my unrealistic expectations about problem-free relationships. Help me understand people instead of trying to change them, and help me love them with my actions.

Boxing Ring

RESOLVING CONFLICTS BY FIGHTING FAIR

LIFE LESSON

When two unique and imperfect people come together, they simply won't agree about everything. That's why it's critical that we learn how to deal effectively with relationship issues.

There should be a special term for conflict in a healthy relationship. *Friendly fire? Care clash? Affection affliction?*

Whatever you call it, dealing with conflict is an important skill to learn, because conflict plays a role in every relationship. Our task, as those who want strong, healthy relationships, is to become experts at fighting fair.

Assuming someone has to lose, the world fights to win. But under God's rules, no one loses because the relationship is more important than who's right or wrong. Conflict dealt with by God's rules draws people closer, because they team up to confront the common enemy—conflict.

■ Describe the attitude you want to cultivate in order to keep the relationship your priority during conflicts.
1 Peter 4:8
Galatians 5:13-16
1 Thessalonians 3:12

■ What makes you sometimes want to avoid a conflict, rather than resolve it?

■ It's loving and courageous to remain committed to the process for as long as resolution takes. What does God's Word say about your reasons for avoidance or escape?
1 Corinthians 13:4-8
Ephesians 4:2-3

The best style of conflict-management is the sparring partner, the person committed to being a teammate and helping his or her partner. Sparring partners stay in the ring and off the ropes. Regardless of how unpleasant it becomes, they stay at it until they come to a mutual decision that they feel is best for both. Sparring partners realize the relationship is more important than anything they could argue about, and they understand that the process is usually more vital than the outcome.

■ Having agreed to fight fair, sparring partners are more likely to achieve lasting peace and resolution. Read these passages and list some of God's techniques for expert conflict-management:
Romans 14:19
2 Timothy 2:22-24
James 3:16-18

■ Becoming an effective sparring partner involves carefully choosing your words. Investigate the Bible's teaching on the sobering power of words for good and for harm:
Proverbs 10:11, 20-21
Proverbs 16:24
Proverbs 18:21

■ Restate some of the following Bible teachings as guidelines for speech in conflict resolution.
Proverbs 10:19
Proverbs 12:18
Proverbs 15:4, 28
Proverbs 16:23
Colossians 4:6

Learn to attack the issues without attacking each other. . . . Instead of attacking, try to own your feelings. If both of you will accept responsibility for your mistakes, then you'll be sparring and growing together rather than wounding and regretting.

"Peace is not the absence of conflict but the presence of creative alternatives for responding to conflict."
—Dorothy Thompson

> *The most important thing you can do is to bring the Prince of Peace into the ring with you.*

■ *Even as Jesus experienced the whole range of emotions He was always directed by His connection to the Father. Describe a few specific ways you want His focus and emotional integrity to rub off on you in your conflicts.*
John 2:13-17
1 Peter 2:21-24
1 John 3:5
Matthew 23

▶ Today's Challenge

You may have more than thirty days to live, but don't let an unresolved conflict tarnish any more of your life. If you need to resolve a conflict with someone, start by gaining a clear understanding of the relational crisis. What is the disagreement really about? What does the other person want? Put yourself in his or her shoes.

Next, pray as you write out what you want to say and what you think the other person might say in response.

Remember, above all, to affirm the other person's value to you. Invite that person to spar as a teammate who, like you, is committed to the relationship.

Plan to meet in person or if necessary by phone, and choose a time and location that feels nonthreatening to both of you.

After you set up the appointment, recruit someone to pray for the conversation.

▶ Face Time

Father, You have given us ample instruction on how to get along. Help me release my ego and my own desires in situations that present conflict. Help me remember that a quality connection with You and with those You've placed in my life is the most important consideration.

Help me stay close to You every day, so Your heart for people will guide the way.

Sandpaper

SMOOTHING THE EDGES

LIFE LESSON

Sandpaper people are part of God's plan for your life. He allows sandpaper people into your life so He can craft you into a sharper tool for His purposes. Paul explains, "For we are God's workmanship, created in Christ Jesus to do good works, which God prepared in advance for us to do" (Ephesians 2:10). In the Greek, the word for "workmanship" literally means "a work of art or a masterpiece." God is crafting you into the perfect tool to accomplish His amazing plan for you.

Tools have an intended purpose. You might notice this best if you attempt to drive a nail with a handsaw or cut a board with a screwdriver. You'll fail to accomplish your task, and likely wind up causing more harm than good.

A nail might desire something softer than a hammer. The board might be afraid of those sharp, scary teeth of the saw. But to serve their purpose for the carpenter, the nail and the board will have to get over their fears.

Likewise, when you need help with your integrity problem, you might not find yourself dealing with someone whose gift is mercy. And when God is teaching you patience, you may not be dealing with the gentlest or most easygoing person.

Today, it's time to overcome your natural fear of God's tools in your life and the sometimes uncomfortable tasks they're intended to perform. Overcoming this fear will, in turn, allow you to be a constructive tool in others' lives.

■ What kind of tools has God been using in your life? What types of tasks do you feel those people or situations are serving in His plan for you?

■ What could you do to cooperate better with some of God's methods for crafting you into the perfect tool?
2 Timothy 2:20-21
2 Timothy 3:16-17
Hebrews 10:24
Hebrews 13:20-21

If we are not only to tolerate but to grow in our sandpaper relationships, then we need to gain the Carpenter's perspective on people and performance. We have to learn to see the difficult people in our lives in a new light.

■ Even people who are behaving badly toward you can serve God's purpose. Think about a few such people you know. Brainstorm a few Jesus-style responses to them. (Consider Galatians 6:1-5 and Proverbs 26:4-5.)

> *If I forget about trying to change everybody else and simply work on letting God change me, then the people in my life are much more open to me.*

■ *Examination of yourself must come before confrontation of others. In John 8:3-11, what do you learn about Jesus' perspective on this principle?*

■ *How does King David model this "me-first" principle? See Psalm 51:9-13.*

"It is impossible for a man to learn what he thinks he already knows."

—Epictetus

> *God is much more interested in our character than in our comfort.*
>
> ■ *Why should becoming like Jesus be your top priority as you consider your spiritual growth?*
>
> ■ *Look at how the apostle Paul clarifies God's purpose and methods in crafting a Jesus-shaped character in you:*
> *Romans 8:29-30*
> *Ephesians 4:22-24*
> *2 Corinthians 3:18*

■ *Late in King David's reign, one of his adult sons attempted a coup and drove David out of Jerusalem. Read 2 Samuel 16:5-13 and imagine yourself in David's place. How would you have responded to the offending son?*

■ *Think of a person who irritates you, and imagine how David might respond to that person if he were in your place. What might David say to himself? to his advisors? to your bothersome acquaintance?*

"The most successful people are those who are good at plan B."

—James Yorke

▶ Today's Challenge

Think about your rough edges. You might be able to see them for yourself, or you might depend on what others have told you. Take a moment to describe a couple of areas you need to have sanded down.

Consider what types of tools would be best for that sanding. For ideas, review our list on pages 96–98 of *One Month to Live*. Has God already placed some of these tools in your life? If so, pray for wisdom about how to cooperate with the work He is doing in you. Write down any insights that come to you.

Who might be a useful tool in your life? Or what type of person? Don't go looking for problems, but find someone whom God might use to bring you balance and maturity.

What's the first action you will take?

▶ Face Time

God, this is hard to say, but thank You for [fill in the person's name] _____. He/she drives me crazy, but I trust You and Your purposes. Please give me patience. Help me accept our differences and, when necessary, to forgive.

Remind me of the times I've irritated You and others so I will be more humble and accepting of this person. And, yes, even grateful for them.

The Gift

THANKING THOSE AROUND YOU

LIFE LESSON

When we are thankful, we become content and full of the peace that only He can provide. Focusing on how grateful we are for what we have prevents us from becoming bitter and greedy for more.

How we see God, life's obstacles, our future hope, or our present circumstances depends largely on where we focus our attention—on the negative or the positive. Do we *choose* to see the people and circumstances in our lives as blessings or as problems?

Some vision problems require corrective lenses. That's why God gives us His Word and His Spirit to aid the eyes of our hearts. Some vision problems are helped by exercises, which is why God commands us to choose to live out attitudes of trust, hope, acceptance, and gratitude.

The bottom line: Abundant life requires recognizing what we have.

> *"Gratitude is not only the greatest of virtues, but the parent of all the others."*
> —Cicero

■ *Although we have cause to be thankful for all of God's blessings, large and small, what are some of our biggest reasons for gratitude?*
Romans 6:17-18
1 Corinthians 15:55-57
Colossians 1:10-14
Revelation 11:16-17

■ *Why is giving thanks to people important?*
How does it relate to giving thanks to God?

"As we express our gratitude, we
must never forget that the highest
appreciation is not to utter words,
but to live by them."

—*John F. Kennedy*

There is power in gratitude to heal us
spiritually, emotionally, and relationally.
An attitude of gratitude opens up our
hearts to God, enabling us to really see the
world the way it is, to experience life to its
fullest and enjoy each breath.

Gratitude can increase our capacity to
love. . . . We become fully aware of the
details of the life we love, the simple
things that delight us, and, perhaps most
of all, the people God has placed in our
lives. Simply stated, gratitude expands our
capacity to enjoy life.

■ *What differences can gratitude make in*
your life?
Psalm 50:23
Ephesians 5:3-4
Philippians 4:6-7

■ In everyday, practical terms, what can you do to put into practice some of the Bible's instructions and examples about how to express your gratitude?
Psalm 100
Ephesians 5:18-20
Philippians 1:3
Colossians 3:17
1 Thessalonians 5:16-18

■ In the Bible, one important component of thanksgiving to God is the idea of making God's actions and character qualities known to others. (See 1 Chronicles 16:7-10; Psalm 35:18; 75:1; and Isaiah 12:1-6.)

■ Who do you want to thank by telling someone else about him/her? Who will you tell? What will you say?

Maybe 10 percent of the people in the world today are fully alive. They truly appreciate the gifts God has given them, and their eyes are wide open to the sacred gift of life. They celebrate each new day and are deeply grateful to God for it. They take advantage of every breath, every moment, and every opportunity to celebrate life.

"Let us be grateful to people who make us happy; they are the charming gardeners who make our souls blossom."

—Marcel Proust

_____

_____

_____

_____

_____

_____

_____

_____

_____

_____

_____

_____

_____

_____

_____

_____

▌ Today's Challenge

Read Psalm 107 and write out your own addition to the psalmist's expressions of praise. What does your own story show about the way God has guided your life? Once you've written your response to God for His work in your life, share your story with someone, as a further expression of thanks to God. You may be surprised by the results.

▌ Face Time

Father, I know how good it makes me feel when someone is truly grateful for something I've given them or done for them. I feel appreciated, valued, wanted.

I want to make You feel that way more often. I'm sorry for my ingratitude. Open my eyes and adjust my focus. Sensitize my heart to Your many blessings.

So many people bless me in so many ways . . . every day. Please help me remember to give them the gift of gratitude a lot more than I have been.

Last Call
REVEALING YOUR HEART

LIFE LESSON

People talk all the time but rarely seem to hear each other's words, let alone their unspoken messages. . . . We have to be willing to move from communication breakdown to communication breakthrough.

A ll real connection involves two-way communication—both speaking and listening. If only half of this is happening, then the communication is not complete. Responses can't be returned. Misperceptions can't be checked and corrected. The speaker doesn't even know whether the listener is receiving the message. When a communication system is not functioning fully, it has to be fixed.

We have to risk vulnerability to the point of possible rejection.

■ What do we learn about God's heart from Jesus that we couldn't know any other way?
John 14:7-11
Hebrews 1:1-3

■ What do people close to you need to see in you—or what do you need them to see—that can only come out as you share your time and troubles?

■ How did people know God was listening to them in these situations?
Exodus 3:6-10
2 Chronicles 7:13-14
Psalm 106:43-45

■ How can you demonstrate to people who share with you that you've really listened to their heart?
Romans 12:15
Philippians 2:3-4

We must be willing to tell the truth but also to temper it with grace. When you're angry, you need to talk about it. When you feel hurt, you need to talk about it. When you have a strong opinion, you need to share it. But how you share the truth can be just as important as the words themselves.

■ *In* One Month to Live, *we quoted Ephesians 4:15. Read that verse's surrounding context (verses 11-16). In your own words, describe what happens in relationships when we speak the truth in love. (See also Ephesians 4:29.)*

■ *According to Jesus, why is it important for you to take quick action to repair damage you've done to a relationship? See Matthew 5:21-24.*

■ *Read Matthew 18:10-17 and think about why these teachings are placed together. With what attitudes does Jesus say we are to go about fixing a relationship that someone else has damaged?*

When we remember that our days are numbered, we realize we don't have time to waste on anything that's not true. In relationships the stakes are just too high to beat around the bush, talk behind someone's back, or not speak honestly. You gain respect when you speak directly.

❯ Today's Challenge

Choose one relationship in which you'd like to improve your two-way, open-hearted communication. Maybe it's your relationship with your spouse, your parents your children, or a friend. It might be a damaged relationship, or maybe it's a good relationship you'd like to make great.

Diagnose the aspects of openness that need improvement. Do you or the other person need to share more openly? Do either or both of you need to listen more genuinely and actively? What needs repair (an offense, a disagreement, apathy), or bolstering (security, trust)? Ask God for His wisdom as you diagnose the relationship's weaknesses.

Now choose one step toward repairing or improving that connection. It's okay to take action regarding something the other person needs to fix, and doing so will involve prayer, preparation, and a humble approach. But look at your own responsibilities first. What's one step you will take toward a more open-hearted relationship?

Take it.

❯ Face Time

God, I'm amazed that You're so personal with us. Your heart is laid bare, and I know You often feel pain because of the risk You've taken. I'm sorry I've hurt You.

Your vulnerability makes possible the miraculous relationship between You and me. Show me how to enjoy that privilege even a fraction as much as You do.

Help me take risks in my relationships with the important people in my life, so we can both enjoy a little glimpse of heaven on earth.

Relationship Evaluation Checklist

❑ I have a relationship with Jesus and a deepening understanding of God's love.

❑ God's love has recently helped me overcome a relational obstacle.

❑ My confidence in God's forgiveness is increasing.

❑ I've genuinely forgiven at least one person in the recent past.

❑ Others will tell you that I'm usually an accepting person.

❑ Others have noticed my loving actions.

❑ I've recently seen one conflict all the way through to a healthy resolution.

❑ I'm consistently remembering to pray during conflicts.

❑ I'm learning to accept an irritating person as God's tool in my life.

❑ At least once recently I've humbly examined my own heart first before confronting someone.

❑ My friends have noticed that I have a positive attitude.

❑ I often say thanks to God and to people.

❑ I'm pretty good at sharing my true thoughts and feelings in a tactful way.

❑ When someone talks to me, that person knows I'm listening carefully.

This self-evaluation may help you identify areas for focused development in your life—not necessarily the "most important" areas, but the ones you think God is prompting you to pursue in the coming months. Look back over Days 9 through 15 and choose applications from one or two of your "Live It Up" exercises that you'd like to build into your life. Write them under "Principle 2" in "My Maximum Life Plan" on page 164.

One Month to Live Lifestyle
Complete Ways to Love

How can we love? We won't even *try* to count the ways. Here's a fresh batch of ideas for putting Week 2 principles into practice. Use them, change them, or come up with creative ideas of your own.

Love Passages
Love Trumps Sin
Psalm 32:1-2
Proverbs 17:9
Romans 12:16-17

Forgiveness
Proverbs 19:11
Matthew 18:21-22
Ephesians 3:11-12
Ephesians 4:32-5:2

Relational Mountains
Proverbs 15:23
Romans 12:18
Philippians 2:1-4
James 1:19-20

Fighting Fair
Proverbs 10:12
John 13:34-35
Hebrews 2:17-18
1 Peter 1:22-23

God's Tools
Psalm 51:10
2 Corinthians 9:8
2 Peter 3:9

Applications requiring a few minutes.

◆ Call or e-mail someone you haven't heard from in a long time.

◆ Brainstorm a list of ten simple ways you can make a quality connection with a loved one.

◆ Think of three good qualities of someone you're angry with and consider telling him or her about these traits that you appreciate.

◆ Did someone recently make you angry? Think of some questions you could have asked that might have helped you see that person's words or actions differently.

◆ Give a hug or compliment to someone who needs it.

◆ During your next conflict, ask for a ten-minute time-out to cool down. Then come back and, for five minutes, try simply to listen and understand.

◆ E-mail or talk to someone you're at odds with just to affirm your commitment to that person and to your relationship.

◆ What people in your life remind you of different tools—such as sandpaper, a hammer, or a vise? Consider how God might be using those people for good purposes in your life.

◆ Spend five minutes prayerfully reflecting on a recent criticism you received. What can you learn from it?

◆ Take a walk through your home, neighborhood, or workplace. Look for evidence of small blessings from God as well as from people.

◆ Write or call someone to say thanks for something he or she has done, said, or meant to you.

◆ If someone were to ask you right now, "How are you?" what would be a more honest answer than "Fine"?

◆ Think of a way to ask, "How are you?" so that the other person understands that you really want to know.

Gratitude
Colossians 2:6-7
Colossians 3:12-16
Philemon 1:4-5
Hebrews 12:28-29

Sharing and Listening
2 Chronicles 7:15-16
Psalm 28:6-7
1 John 1:1-3

Day Jobs

Applications that take an hour or so . . .

The Most Important Relationship

If you have questions about what it means to start a close relationship with Jesus, talk to someone from a church that takes the Bible seriously. Or someone who consistently lives the life described in this book. Read Day 29 in *One Month to Live* to learn more about God's love for you.

Know Your Style

Talk with at least two people who know you fairly well. Pray beforehand for the ability to listen nondefensively. Explain to them the various fighting styles described in Day 12 and ask them which of these they've seen you use. Also ask them specifically what you do or say in the heat of an argument. Thank them for their honesty and then use their feedback to determine at least one new way you'll become a better sparring partner. Plan how to practice that skill.

Pre-Confrontation Conditioning

Lovingly confronting others about blind spots or sin is an important service we offer, but we should never do so without genuine humility and love. If you think God wants you to have such a conversation with someone, first spend at least a half hour reading God's Word and praying. Examine your heart for ways you've committed either the same offenses that the other person has, or offenses just as significant. Talk with God about your own imperfections and His loving acceptance of you.

Then spend some time praying to have God's heart of love and acceptance for the other person. Pray for a genuine desire for that person's best—that he or she would feel affirmed and would receive your words as well-intentioned and helpful insights.

Sixty Minutes

Spend an *extra* hour with someone important to you. Yes, an hour in addition to your normal time together. During that time, do an activity you both enjoy, but one that allows you to talk and listen to each other. Be prepared to share one meaningful issue that makes you feel vulnerable. If the other person shares, use questions ("How did that make you feel?") and words of empathy ("I'm sorry. That had to hurt.") to make sure he or she knows you're listening.

Time Release

Applications to be completed over days or weeks.

Change "Me First" to "You First"

Choose someone important in your life—your spouse, friend, parent, child, sibling, fellow worker, teacher, or neighbor. Set up an interview at a private, distraction-free time and place. Your purpose is simply to learn to see more clearly through that person's eyes, to understand what makes him or her tick.

Write out your questions ahead of time: What do you dream about being or doing? What do you think and feel about the world and the people around you? What makes you happy or excited? What makes you sad, angry, or scared? What do people do or say that makes you feel loved and accepted? What makes you feel rejected? And so on.

Record your interview. Review it and take notes later. Come up with several new ways to put that person first in your interactions in the future. You might, for instance, choose activities to do his way, words that are affirming to her, preferences you'll honor, and topics you'll listen to.

From Attitude to Gratitude

Choose something you often complain about. Take some time to pray and think about it from different angles. How important is it, really? Is the annoying action being done with good intentions? Or is it something the guilty party is not even aware of doing? If the issue is no human's fault—such as weather or a health issue—what good might God be bringing out of this, for you or for others? What in your life is still good *in spite of* this?

Jot down a short list of blessings you want to start habitually thanking God and people for. This doesn't mean you stop trying to change the problem, if it can be changed, but this practice will mean you'll live with a healthier attitude. Carry your list with you or put it where you'll see it regularly. When you feel like complaining, choose instead to thank God (or someone else) for something specific. Focus on this new habit for several days or weeks.

Principle 3

Learn Humbly

If you're a Jesus-follower, then you're in school. Your major? Beginning, intermediate, and advanced Jesus-following, of course.

In this school, you don't just fill your head; you change your heart.

You don't just get smarter; you become more mature.

Rather than testing what you know, you're tested in order to grow.

And when you fail, your Teacher throws out the test.
(Someone Else took it for you a long time ago. He aced it . . .
and that means you did too.)

In this school, you learn about God and about yourself—who He made you to be and what He created you to do. With growing awareness, you begin the inner transformation that will make you the best *you* that you can be in Jesus Christ.

Star Power

DISCOVERING WHO YOU WERE MEANT TO BE

LIFE LESSON

To know our purpose in life, we must learn who we are, and we do that by recognizing whose we are. Our purpose and identity grow clearer as we come to know God better.

Throughout the Bible, one important word that keeps popping up is *remember*. It makes sense that God would place this word prominently and repeatedly in His message to the amnesiac human race.

We forget a lot of things. But we'd remember many of them if we'd just hang onto one answer to one question: *Who am I?*

It's strange that even we who have become God's children should be so prone to forget our identity. If you or I were the child of a president or king or famous actor or author, you'd think we'd remain constantly aware of our heritage, even if we wanted to avoid publicity. Maybe our memory loss is because 100-percent-forgiven-child-of-the-Creator is simply hard for us to believe.

■ *Do you think remembering your identity would be easier if you believed more firmly that you are a 100-percent-forgiven child of the Creator? What could you do to become better convinced?*

God says to you and me today, "Remember who you are. You are My child. You are a child of the King."

■ To understand your identity, listen to what your generous and inventive Creator said in Ephesians 1:3-14. Start a dossier on yourself based on this passage.

■ What are your favorite three realities about yourself mentioned in Ephesians 1:3-14? Why?

Identity theft is . . . our enemy's number one strategy. . . . While God's purpose is to bring you life to the fullest, Satan has a plan for you to settle for so much less than what you were made for. . . . He knows if he can steal your identity, he will destroy your dreams and your purpose in life.

"Satan" is one of our enemy's names, used in both the Old and New Testaments. It means "adversary, accuser." In New Testament Greek, he's also called the "devil" (*diabolos*), which means "slanderer, false accuser." Both are used in Revelation 12:9-10.

■ Satan uses the same ammo over and over, but he tailors each bullet to its individual victim. Write a list of the lies he has custom-designed for you to ensure your maximum memory loss.

■ Use these or other passages (like Ephesians 1:3-14 above) to come up with God's antidotes for some or all of the lies you just listed. Personalize these verses. After all, they're God's words to you.
John 1:11-13
Galatians 3:26; 4:4-7
1 John 3:1-3

■ What can you do to fix God's truths about you firmly in your memory? Consider ideas from James 4:7; 1 Peter 5:8-9; and 1 John 2:1-2.

God repeatedly and emphatically tells us, "You mean so much to me. I have a grand purpose for your life. I had a specific reason for creating you exactly as I did."

■ *Why can you be confident that you can
discover God's special purpose for you?*
Psalm 25:12
Philippians 2:13

*We can all learn more about who God
made us to be by focusing on Him. As we
develop a closer relationship with God,
we become more like Him, thwarting our
Enemy's attempts to steal our identity.*

▌ Today's Challenge

Find, buy, or create something that will remind you of your identity. Choose a
symbolic object, a bookmark, a poster . . . Paint a picture, create a collage, make a
video . . . Write a poem, record a song, create a personalized identity dictionary, or
whatever.

Think ahead about how you will use it as a daily reminder. Will you hang it on
your wall, put it inside the novel you're currently reading, make it your alarm in the
morning, attach it to your key ring?

▌ Face Time

Father . . . It's so cool to call You that. I'm so grateful You chose to make me Your
child.

A lot of the time I'm overwhelmed by that fact.

But sometimes I don't remember that I'm Yours—or maybe I don't want to
remember. Help me in my unbelief. Help me see what it is in me—my doubts and
selfish values—that resists remembering whose I am. And help me conquer those, so
I'll never forget You're my Father.

GPS
FINDING YOUR DIRECTION

| LIFE LESSON | *God provides our life's direction by means of our gifts, passions, and struggles.* |

God's will is our perfect guide in life (see Romans 12:2). He makes it available, but we have to find it. He puts on our shoulders the responsibility to seek His will and make choices to go His way in His strength.

Among the signposts that point us along our unique life paths are our

Gifts

Passions

Struggles

God's GPS. So let's get oriented. Now.

"Who, then, is the man that fears the LORD? He will instruct him in the way chosen for him." (Psalm 25:12)

■ *We're all experts at something, and no one excels at everything.*

■ Many people have times when they doubt that God's forgiveness is deep enough to cover everything, forever. In your own words, write a letter to yourself from God, based on the truth found in these passages:
Ephesians 1:7-8
Hebrews 4:14-16
Hebrews 8:12
1 John 5:11-15

■ How completely do you accept God's forgiveness? Do you usually believe it's real, or do you live in persistent skepticism?

■ When someone forgives you, do you feel relief? Or do you keep beating yourself up?

■ How does your ability to accept forgiveness influence your willingness to extend forgiveness to others?

If you try to live without forgiving, you won't survive. It is essential that we forgive for our own sakes; otherwise we'll drown in bitterness.

■ What do you think are some of your special gifts or talents? How do these help you discern God's direction for your life?

■ You can learn a lot about the gifts and talents God gives us from Romans 12:3-8 and 1 Corinthians 12.

When you pursue the passions God has placed in your heart, He simply loves it. . . . He finds so much joy in your living out your giftedness and being who He created you to be. We not only feel fulfilled as we live from our passions, but we sense God's pleasure as well.

"A life spent making mistakes is not only more honorable, but more useful than a life spent doing nothing."
—George Bernard Shaw

■ Read Titus 2:11-14, noting the final phrase. How does God transform His followers' passions from immoral to God-honoring?

■ If you maintain one central passion for God, you'll have little problem keeping your other, personalized passions focused correctly. What can you do to cultivate the enthusiasm for God described in these passages?
Psalm 27:4
Psalm 42:1-2
Psalm 63:1-8
Jeremiah 29:13

■ What are some of your personal passions? (Proverbs 2:1-11; Acts 2:42; 17:11; 1 Corinthians 16:15; and Titus 3:14 give a few ideas.) How do your passions help you discern God's direction for you?

You have creative license to be who God made you to be. The great theologian Dr. Seuss once said, "Be who you are because those who mind don't matter and those who matter don't mind."

*T*he third component of God's GPS is our struggles. God often takes our struggles, pain, and problems and uses them to guide us to our purpose. This is such an important topic that we're going to explore it in detail on Days 18 and 20.

_____

_____

_____

_____

_____

_____

_____

_____

_____

_____

▶ Today's Challenge

Take what you've learned about your gifts and passions (and your struggles, if you already have some insights) and look for any patterns that might clarify God's direction for your life—or at least for this moment in your life. Do the GPS components have any points of connection? anything in common? Do they somehow work together to make you lean toward a particular cause or activity or job or ministry?

If you think you're discerning some possible direction, choose one experimental step to take in that direction. Often we confirm God's direction simply by doing—by trying something and using the experience to recalibrate our GPS reading.

Take that step. Or do whatever it takes to get ready for it.

▶ Face Time

God, You're so good not to leave me directionless. You're so wise to build a GPS unit right into me and my circumstances. Now help me understand Your direction for me.

Guide me in finding and using my gifts for Your purpose. Stir the passions that You planted in me and let them empower me toward Your goals for my life. And help me accept my struggles as refining tools to make me who I'm meant to be.

Hurricanes
WITHSTANDING THE WINDS OF CHANGE

LIFE LESSON

In life, difficult change is inevitable; half of our battle is learning to accept that reality. The other half is seeking God's wisdom for dealing with each storm.

We can't prevent the hurricane winds of change. . . . But we can prepare for them and learn from prior storms.

Job 5:7—Man is born to trouble as surely as sparks fly upward.

James 4:14-15—You do not even know what will happen tomorrow. What is your life? You are a mist that appears for a little while and then vanishes. Instead, you ought to say, "If it is the Lord's will, we will live and do this or that."

1 Peter 4:12—Dear friends, do not be surprised at the painful trial you are suffering, as though something strange were happening to you.

When God allows us to go through struggles, problems, and difficulties, we learn to depend on Him. We learn our own limits and are reminded to look to Him for what we need most. As we learn to depend upon Him, He fills us with His power and His strength.

"Yet, in the maddening maze of things,
And tossed by storm and flood,
To one fixed stake my spirit clings;
I know that God is good!"
—*John Greenleaf Whittier*

■ Why are difficulties in our lives so valuable?
James 1:2-4
1 Peter 1:6-9
Romans 5:3-4

■ According to these passages, what can you do to cooperate with God's purposes in your hardships?

The winds of change will either make you stronger or knock you down. . . . By putting biblical principles into practice, we'll see that we can not only survive the winds of change, but we can harness them to fill our sails and propel us forward.

*Paul chose to look beyond the raging
waters and gale-force winds to an
upcoming, positive change. Human nature
inclines us to look only at the immediate
problem and its collateral damage.*

■ What will we see when we learn to take
the long view and look past the storm?
Proverbs 10:25
Matthew 7:24-27
John 16:19-22
Galatians 6:9-10
Hebrews 10:35-37

■ How do you want this perspective to
impact your response to change and difficulty?
Be specific.

■ Jesus traveled lightly. He kept only the
cargo that was most important for His health
and His mission. He advised His followers to
do the same. What is your response to His
advice? What cargo might Jesus want to you
discard from your life?
Matthew 6:19-21
Mark 10:28-31

*Even when you don't feel His presence, God
is still with you. He's behind the storm, in
the midst of the storm, and beyond the
storm, always there waiting for you, ever
present.*

■ Based on these passages, create a reminder that God never changes even though everything else does.
Numbers 23:19
Deuteronomy 32:3-4
Psalm 102:25-28

■ Why is this conviction helpful as you face a present storm or anticipate a future one?

"When we are no longer able to change a situation, we are challenged to change ourselves."

—Victor Frankl

■ Are you in a storm now? If so, describe your thoughts and feelings.

■ Read these promises from God, your reliable Navigator. Then talk to Him about your circumstances and your attitudes.
Psalm 116:1-8
John 16:33
1 Corinthians 1:8-9
Isaiah 46:9-11

"Things alter for the worse spontane-
ously, if they be not altered for the better
designedly."

—Francis Bacon

▌Today's Challenge

How has your faith sustained you through some of the storms in the past? With the most recent storm in mind, what did you learn from it about yourself? What did you learn about God? Spend some time in prayer, connecting with your Anchor, thanking Him for the ways He has sustained you and will continue to hold you firmly.

▌Face Time

God, where are You? I can't hear or see or feel You. Please show me, somehow, that You're there and that You really are in charge. It's okay if You don't yank me out of this storm (although I won't put up a fuss if You do), but at least give me the assurance that You'll bring me through, and that this crazy, scary, confusing time serves a good purpose.

In Your strength, I can handle anything, as long as I know there's a reason for it. Even if I don't know the reason.

Metamorphosis
CHANGING FROM THE INSIDE OUT

LIFE LESSON

If you elevate status symbols, then you're really trying to give the appearance of a healthy, well-balanced, successful life without the reality of it. You're trying to change from the outside in, thinking you will feel better about yourself on the inside if you change your settings and props on the outside. We think, If I change my looks, if I change my house, if I change my car, then it's going to change me. Then I will truly be content. *Only one problem: it doesn't work.*

Some of the "virtues" that our world endorses—busy-ness, power, one-upmanship, the easy life—can quickly become dis-eases of the soul, when we count on them to give us real satisfaction, real life. And we know something's wrong.

Abundant life is only found as we cultivate internal maturity in constant connection with God. But the paths that lead to the metamorphosis of the soul are unpopular and not often traveled.

> *Too often we wait on someone or something external to change us. . . . It's time to take responsibility for our own growth.*

■ In your everyday life, what are some specific ways you can take responsibility for your internal transformation?
2 Corinthians 3:18
2 Corinthians 4:6-7
Ephesians 4:22-24

Motion and commotion steal the soul, but stillness restores the soul.

■ What kinds of "motion" do you want to replace with stillness, at least some of the time? How will this change you inside?
Psalm 37:7-8
Psalm 62:1-2
Psalm 131:1-3
Isaiah 30:15

The quickest way to suffocate our souls is to try to control everything. . . . If we stop trying to solve all our problems and to control everything, quietness will fill our souls with strength.

"Most of the evils of life arise from man's inability to sit still in a room."

—Blaise Pascal

■ What did Jesus do to teach and model silence and solitude? How did these practices help Him depend on His Father's control?
Matthew 6:6
Matthew 26:36-39
Mark 1:35
Luke 6:12-13

■ Read the following teachings of Jesus, then write an e-mail to Jesus responding to His challenge. Or record a voice mail. Or just go respond with action.
Matthew 20:25-28
Matthew 25:31-40
John 13:12-17

God doesn't want to waste a hurt. He wants us to endure with grace, and we do that by trusting Him. Grace is the power to change—not what we can do for ourselves but what God does for and through us.

"There is no exercise better for the heart than reaching down and lifting people up."

—John Andrew Holmes

■ A lot of the time the apostle Paul was one very uncomfortable man. In his eyes, why was the physical pain worth it?
2 Corinthians 4:8-11, 16-18
2 Corinthians 6:3-10

■ What costly comfort are you clinging to? What priceless pain are you working overtime to avoid?

■ By the power of God's grace, how will your struggles help you soar?

▶ Today's Challenge

You'll be wise to eventually make these habits—stillness, silence, and suffering—part of your daily lifestyle. But God changes us by degrees.

If you haven't done so already, decide on one specific way you could practice each of these habits. Then choose one to start today or tomorrow. Take some step now to ensure that you'll follow through—schedule the activity, call someone for accountability and support, acquire a resource for the activity, or all of the above.

▶ Face Time

Yuck, Lord. I hate discipline. But I love You. And I know You promise that the work will be worth it. So give me the strength and commitment to stick with it, at least as long as it takes for me to start seeing and feeling the benefits. Please enrich my experience of You . . . soon. I need the encouragement.

Earthquake
BUILDING A FOUNDATION THAT LASTS

LIFE LESSON

Major losses are inevitable in life, but with a strong spiritual foundation we can remain standing and grow stronger.

God never abandons us. He suffers right along with us and knows more than anyone what it means to lose a child, to be rejected by His people, to be betrayed by a friend.

■ *If you were convinced that someone genuinely empathized and grieved with you through all of your greatest losses, what difference would that make for you?*

If you have anything other than God at the center of your life when the earthquake of problems hits, your center won't be strong enough to hold you together.

■ *Why is God the only suitable center for your life? What are some practical ways you can push aside any competitors and make and keep God central?*
Colossians 3:1-5
1 Timothy 6:17-19
1 Samuel 2:2-8
Isaiah 44:6-9

God designed us to live in community, gladly offering help when others need it and gracefully accepting help when we are in need.

"Faith is the sturdiest, the most manly of the virtues. It lies behind our pluck-iest . . . strivings. It is the virtue of the storm, just as happiness is the virtue of the sunshine."

—Ruth Benedict

■ Why do need to stay connected with fellow
Jesus-followers?
Acts 2:41-47
Acts 4:32-35
Romans 12:15
Hebrews 10:24-25

■ What do you miss out on when you're
disconnected? Why is this so dangerous?

How do you know if God is truly the center
of your life? You stop worrying!

"This is what I found out about religion:
it gives you courage to make decisions
you must make in a crisis and then the
confidence to leave the result to a Higher
Power. Only by trust in God can a man
carrying responsibility find repose."
—Dwight D. Eisenhower

> ■ *King David endured some terrifying times, especially early in his life. After God brought him through one especially harrowing episode, David wrote a song about it. Read at least part of his song—in 2 Samuel 22:1-18, 31-32. As you prepare for and then endure your next earthquake, what can you do to cultivate the knee-jerk reaction to pray first?*
>
> ■ *How does spending time with God and in His word affect your attitude?*

*I*n the middle of a lifequake, we scream out to God for rescue, for relief, for an end to the noise and shaking.

But God is wisely, lovingly selective about which blessings He grants us, and when He grants them. Don't be surprised if the quake continues, and you're still scared.

One thing you can always know: God has already granted you His greatest blessing—Himself. His presence with you at all time, through all circumstances.

And His amazing gift is a package deal. When He promises His presence, He is automatically assuring you that . . .

He knows,

He understands,

He cries,

He guides,

He heals,

and He changes us.

▌ **Today's Challenge**

Identify one loss that you're either going through now or that you fear might come your way. Take a few minutes to talk honestly with God about it.

Now, keeping in mind that He's still there with you, choose one of the ideas from this chapter for strengthening your trust in God. What, specifically, do you want to do to make this happen? What do you yourself need to invest? What can you only count on God for? In what ways do other Jesus-followers need to be involved?

Write or record your thoughts. Share your plan with at least one other person. Then keep hanging onto God as you take that first step.

▌ **Face Time**

Almighty God, I want You solidly at the center of my life, and I want You all around me—as my Foundation and my Fortress. Teach me to love everything I need to do in order to make that happen. Help me to see You in the process, not just at the end.

And there, in the middle of You, show me how to become vulnerably, victoriously interdependent with Your people. Squash my selfish pride and tenderize my heart toward Your community.

Mulligan
PLAYING WITH INTEGRITY

LIFE LESSON

If you only had one month to live, most likely you would want to review your life and examine your character. You would want to do all you could to learn from the mistakes in your past, iron out any wrinkles that had developed, and live your remaining days at peace. You would want your life to be integrated and whole, not compartmentalized and fragmented as we often experience when we're going through the motions of life and settling for less than we were made to enjoy. If you were living deliberately and passionately and were fully alive, you would want to live with integrity.

Integrity is the opposite of image. Integrity is when your private life matches your public image. When what you see is what you get—that's integrity. Integrity is who you are when no one is looking.

■ Read about Jesus' confrontation with the hypocritical leaders in Matthew 23:1-7, 23-28. If you notice any parallels between their divided living and yours, ask God's forgiveness and then talk with Him about ways to better align your saying and your doing.

■ What might you do to follow the example of Samuel in 1 Samuel 3:19-20? What would it mean if none of your words "fell to the ground"?

"Dear Christ, make one that which we are and that which we appear to be. Be Lord of naked faces."

—Calvin Miller

If you risk loving, then you'll tell the truth. The more you love, the more you have the courage to tell the truth.

God keeps the scorecard, and it's accurate.
We're not going to come close to His perfect
score. But . . . for each of us, if we're
willing to accept the gift of relationship
with Him, Jesus replaces our scorecards
with His. Then with Jesus' perfect scorecard
in hand, we face God as He welcomes us.

"The strength of a man's virtue should not
be measured by his special exertions, but
by his habitual acts."

—Blaise Pascal

■ Why are both living truthfully and
speaking truthfully necessary components of
imitating your Father's love and courage? See
Ephesians 5:8-10.

■ *Read these passages out loud and hear God speaking directly to you. Listen for His heart. What do you see/hear/feel? Respond to His heart as you wish, in whatever way you wish.*

Isaiah 53:4-6
1 Peter 3:18
2 Corinthians 5:21

▶ **Today's Challenge**

What do-over do you wish you could have? Take some time to talk with God about your regret. Ask His forgiveness and thank Him for making forgiveness possible at the price of Jesus' life.

Ask God to give you strength and wisdom so you won't make the same mistake again, and then let Him guide you toward a more perfect "game."

With His help, think of one step you can take today that will improve your integrity in that area of life where you wish you could have a do-over.

Then go do it.

▶ **Face Time**

Father, I'm both scared and glad that You know and see everything because You know when my public image contradicts my private reality. Help me live with greater integrity, not just because I don't want You to see my hypocrisy, but also because I want to have a unified heart like Yours.

Road Signs
EXPERIENCING A PERSONAL MIRACLE

LIFE LESSON

Miracles are not only possible; they're more common than we think. God cares for us and wants to work in our lives. The hard part is remembering this when we come to a crossroads and must choose how to respond.

Throughout the next few pages are references for several Bible stories. The stories all share a similar pattern. In each situation, God wanted to work a miracle for His people. But He wouldn't do His thing until they fulfilled the requirements we've discussed in *One Month to Live,* Day 22.

Read as many of the stories as you wish, and for each one, try to discern the following:

    1. What the people said about their need for God

    2. What God-given resources they made available to Him

    3. What U-turn they made from a negative direction to a positive one

    4. What God did

    5. The ways they shared the blessing of God's miracle with others

Or for each question, note how the people *didn't* fulfill God's requirements and what He did as a result.

Exodus 12:1-39

Exodus 14

Miracles never take place until you acknowledge the situation is impossible without God.

Numbers 13–14

Joshua 3:1–4:18

Joshua 6

Your time, talent, resources, and energy are God's starting place. Your willingness and surrender activate God's intervention and blessings.

Joshua 9

"*All the blessings we enjoy are Divine deposits, committed to our trust on this condition, that they should be dispensed for the benefit of our neighbors.*"
—*John Calvin*

1 Samuel 17

2 Kings 5:1-17

> *Why would God want to bless us if we're
> not willing to bless anyone else? We are
> blessed to be a blessing.*

Jonah 1

Matthew 8:1-13

▌ Today's Challenge

What's something big—something miraculous—that God might be wanting to do in your life? Read through the four road signs in the book—one-way, stop sign, you-turn, and yield—and prayerfully, honestly evaluate how well you've followed through on each one.

It may be that you're doing fine in all but one area, so the door to God's miracle stays shut. If so, then you know what your next stage of growth will involve.

If, however, you find yourself lacking in two or more of these responses to God, your opening-the-door process may have to come in stages. Pick the first stage you will address.

In either case, identify your first step in opening the door for God's miracle. Invite others to encourage and pray for you. And then take the step.

▌ Face Time

Lord, You are so amazing. You're awesome beyond my comprehension—the only Being in all the universe who truly deserves to be called awesome.

Compared to the amazing feats You're willing to perform in my life, what You require of me in the miracle-releasing process is miniscule—embarrassingly tiny.

But honestly, it feels heavy to me, Lord. I'm such a weakling. And I guess that's the point, isn't it? I need You to help me see how much I need You. And then to help me admit that to You. So I invite Your help today, God. Thank You.

Attitude Assessment Checklist

❑ Most of the time I remember and believe I'm God's child.

❑ I'm usually confident that God has a special purpose for me.

❑ I have a pretty good handle on my gifts and what God wants me to do with them.

❑ I can describe my God-given passions and how they are directing my life.

❑ I expect to deal with difficult changes, because they're a reality of life.

❑ I often remember to look beyond my storms to God's good outcome.

❑ My friends can identify ways that I take responsibility for my growth.

❑ I regularly take time for stillness and solitude with God.

❑ During troubled times, I usually turn first to God.

❑ I'm connected with God's community, and I go to His people when I'm hurting.

❑ Those who know me best also know that my private life is the same as my public image.

❑ I'm confident that God sees His Son's perfect character in me and that He accepts me.

❑ I know that God can and will do amazing things in and through my life.

❑ One big reason I want God's miracles is to share the blessings with others.

This self-evaluation may help you identify areas for focused development in your life—not necessarily the "most important" areas, but the ones you think God is prompting you to pursue in the coming months. Look back over Days 16 through 22 and choose applications from one or two of your "Live It Up" exercises that you'd like to build into your life. Write them under "Principle 3" in "My Maximum Life Plan" on page 166.

One Month to Live Lifestyle
Humble Ways to Learn

We all learn in different ways, so no one style or approach works for everyone. We hope you'll find something here that fits you. Or feel free to adapt an idea to your God-given design. The important thing is to keep on learning and growing.

Education Passages

Whose You Are
Romans 8:12-23
1 John 5:18-19
2 Timothy 2:20-21
Zechariah 3:1-2

GPS
1 Timothy 4:14
Galatians 4:18
Matthew 5:14-16
Philippians 2:14-16

Storm Shelter
1 Samuel 15:29
Psalm 33:10-11
Philippians 4:11-13

Transformation
Lamentation 3:21-26
Matthew 5:43-47
Romans 8:29
1 Corinthians 15:47-49

Foundation
Deuteronomy 32:3-4
2 Timothy 1:7-10
2 Timothy 2:19

Quick Takes

Applications requiring a few minutes.

◆ Explain to someone what it means to be God's child.

◆ Write down one of Satan's lies about your identity. Tear up that piece of paper, then write God's answering truth.

◆ Call or e-mail three friends and ask them, "What do I do that really helps people?"

◆ List or illustrate three situations in your life that excite you . . . and three that sadden you, three situations that you wish were different.

◆ Jettison one TV show or dessert and invest the time or money you saved in one of God's priorities.

◆ If you're in a storm, ask God for a weather forecast. Read Hebrews 10:35-36.

◆ Find a place where you'll be undistracted and spend at least ten minutes sitting silently with God, just to prove to yourself that you can do it.

◆ Do a chore for a family member, roommate, or neighbor.

◆ Call another Jesus-follower and ask what that person needs prayer for. Or ask him or her to pray for something you need.

◆ What are you going to do after you finish today's session? Pray about it first.

◆ Make a simple promise and then keep it.

◆ Ask God whether it would be helpful or healing for you to come clean with one person who doesn't know the real you.

◆ If you've been putting off an intimidating task, tell God you need Him in order to do it.

◆ Identify one small step you could take, or one resource you already have, that would help God work a miracle in your life.

Integrity
Proverbs 16:13
Matthew 15:1-20
Romans 3:20-26
Romans 5:6-8

Miracles
2 Peter 1:3-4
Jude 1:24-25
Acts 3–4

Day Jobs

Applications that take an hour or so.

Learning by Doing

The best way to confirm whether or not you have a particular spiritual gift is to try using it. Talk with friends or church leaders about a way you can try out a particular talent in a real ministry situation, maybe in your church or perhaps somewhere else. You'll probably need more than one attempt to know whether you're gifted, but the first step is the hardest. Take that step and see if you enjoy that activity and whether others benefit from your efforts.

An Hour with God

It's okay to plan your time with God. (Just be prepared if He departs from your plan.) Here's one of a million ways to spend an hour with Him:

Ten minutes: Sing or listen to worship music. Read Psalm 145.

Ten minutes: Confession. Unburden your heart to Him.

Thirty minutes: Sit silently. Be aware of God's presence. Write any thoughts that come to mind.

Ten minutes: Thanksgiving. Praise and thank God for anything.

Put your notes away. Pull them out a week later and review them with God to see if any idea you wrote down might be words of guidance or instruction from Him.

Mapping a Miracle

Look at the next steps in pursuing your miracle. (1) Plan how you will stay in an attitude of humble dependence on God. (2) Start a list of resources already available to you. (Don't forget people!) (3) Prayerfully search your heart for negative attitudes and determine how to replace them with God's truth. (4) Plan how you want to share God's blessing with others.

Time Release

Applications to be completed over days or weeks.

Take Your Identity to Heart

In Psalm 119:11, King David wrote to God, "I have hidden your word in my heart." What if God's truth about your identity filled your heart all the time? What if it were engraved so deeply into your being that you always believed it? How would your daily inner and outer life be different?

You *can* memorize God's Word. Students and actors memorize ideas and words all the time. The trick to keeping God's Word fixed in your heart is to understand and value the *meaning* in the words by repeatedly thinking them and praying them. So take from the Bible a short statement of truth about your identity (maybe from a passage listed in Day 16) and write or record it so you can review it again and again. You might choose "He predestined us to be adopted as his sons" from Ephesians 1:5. Read or listen to this one simple statement, pausing to think about each word. "Predestined" . . . *He thought about me long ago . . . He cared long ago . . . He made a plan for me long, long ago.* "Adopted" . . . *He didn't take me because He had to . . . He chose me, on purpose.* "Sons" . . . *I know that's Bible talk for "children," both genders.* And so on.

As you think, also pray. *God, how long ago did You love me? You've had a lot going on throughout history . . . but You still kept me, little me, in Your plans. Thank You.*

Do this for at least one or two brief sessions each day. After a few days, surprise! You'll not only have the words hidden in your heart, but also a lot of significant life meaning. Do this with one short Bible truth, then start on a new one. Go back occasionally and review previous truths to keep them fresh.

Reality Check

Hard times wouldn't be so hard if we didn't expect life to be so easy. Most of us are conditioned to expect a pain-free life. So when we suffer, we think, "This is wrong. This shouldn't be happening." Or we assume we did something to deserve it.

But not all pain is wrong; often it's the best thing that could happen to us. And not all pain is our fault.

Our church has a ministry to believers all over the world who are persecuted for their Christianity. Spend some time reading stories of those who are being persecuted for the faith. If possible, get involved or help start a ministry at your church for those who are being persecuted.

Learn what countless Jesus-followers in much of the world consider to be normal life in Jesus Christ—and also listen to their hearts. They're thrilled to be following Jesus at any cost.

There are values much higher than your comfort. Give yourself a chance to own such values for yourself.

Principle 4

Leave Boldly

You've seen that little stenciled notice on your side view mirror:
"Objects in mirror are closer than they appear."

We all need a reminder like that on our bathroom mirrors,
to see every morning: "Death and eternity are
closer than they appear."

We're not trying to scare you (although some of us need a good
scare). We're trying to give you a reality check, so you can make
decisions today that will avoid feelings of regret in the future.
We're offering a wake-up call that you implied you wanted
when you started reading this book.

On the one hand, we should all feel a sense of urgency about
investing our short days for eternal benefit. On the other hand, be
encouraged: you can accumulate quite a sizable eternal treasure
for God—and you have the rest of your life to do it!

So as we journey together this fourth week, allow yourself
to feel a little adrenaline-concern about investing well.
And at the same time thank God for the amazing opportunities
and resources He will make available to you
from now until you leave this earth.

Sandcastles
CREATING A LASTING LEGACY

LIFE LESSON

How many of us are using our resources to build a permanent foundation beneath our sandcastles? If we truly want to leave an eternally enduring legacy, then we need to look beyond our home, our investment portfolio, and our heirloom jewelry. If we're going to leave a legacy that the waves of time can't wash away, we need to do an on-site inspection of the life we're currently building. We must honestly evaluate the castle we're constructing to make sure it's not made of sinking sand.

My life, my time, is not my own. It belongs to Christ, and it's His name that will last; only when I live to influence others for Him will I leave an enduring legacy.

■ If a friend said to you, "This is my life. I
can do whatever I want with it," what might
be your response OR what would you like your
response to be?
1 Chronicles 29:10-16
Psalm 100:3
Romans 14:7-9
1 Corinthians 4:7
1 Corinthians 6:19-20
2 Corinthians 5:14-15

■ Read 2 Corinthians 8-9. Identify and
summarize some of Paul's arguments for
giving. Try writing it as a "defense of the virtue
of giving."

This may be the greatest secret to leaving a legacy of substance: try to understand what the Lord wants you to do—and do it. Obey God, because He gives you just enough time to do everything you need to do.

"God asks no man whether he will accept life. That is not the choice. You must take it. The only question is how."

—Henry Ward Beecher

■ What obstacles keep you from always obeying God promptly? See Psalm 119:60.

■ What might you do to overcome one of those obstacles?

"To know what has to be done, then do it, comprises the whole philosophy of practical life."

—*Sir William Osler*

▌ Today's Challenge

Imagine that Jesus left behind His written will and testament. You discover it and sit down to read it. You learn to your amazement that, not only are you a beneficiary, but you're included in the will. Jesus has listed your life as one of His assets. And He's given specific instructions as to how your days are to be disbursed.

Write parts of that document's stipulations about how you are to invest your days, hours, and minutes. Include the stipulations you're living out right now.

Choose one new way you'll follow through with Jesus' will today.

▌ Face Time

Jesus, I throw away a lot of Your resources every day. I know I'll never be a perfect steward. But I want to get better and better at consulting You about Your wishes for Your property.

So I'm thinking this is the way You want me to spend the next hour, the next ten dollars, the next relational contact . . . [share your ideas]. I trust You're helping guide my decision. If I'm off course, somehow redirect me, so I can make the most of this part of my life. For You.

Seeds
PLANTING FOR THE FUTURE

LIFE LESSON

Every day, every moment, with every action, you're planting something. So the question is, what exactly are you planting? What is the cumulative effect of your words, actions, and intentions on those around you and those ahead of you? What harvest will be reaped from all that you plant day in and day out? From the outside, it may be difficult to discern between a seed and a pebble. But, of course, inside they're vastly different. There is life in the seed; there is nothing but rock inside the pebble. The seed has power and potential in it; it produces life. Unfortunately, some of us spend our time planting rocks—no potential, no life, no fruit.

"You can give without loving, but you cannot love without giving."
—Leonard Carmichael

■ What did you do this last week that will last for the rest of the year? for ten years? for eternity? Read the parable of the sower in Matthew 13. Which type of soil describes your heart at the moment?

People are created in God's image as spiritual beings who will live for eternity, either with Him or apart from Him. If we invest in people's lives, then our legacy becomes like a giant oak, providing life for generations to come.

The crucial test in determining if we're planting real seeds or just rocks emerges in our motivation for planting. Am I sowing seed to meet my own needs or to meet the needs of others?

"To know even one life has breathed easier because you have lived. This is the meaning of success."
—*Ralph Waldo Emerson*

■ Read John 12:24. What selfish desires have you had to die to in order to live for God?

▌ Today's Challenge

Plant a small tree or a flower in your yard or a friend's yard as a reminder to you to always invest in the lives of others. Have a conversation with a friend about the legacy you would like to leave on this earth.

▌ Face Time

Lord, I want my life—every minute of it—to count for eternity. Why does it sometimes feel like such a chore to fulfill the greatest privilege in the universe—to serve You with all I have? Maybe if it were easy, though, I wouldn't have to depend on You.

So here I am. Show me how to invest eternal seeds as I go about my days. And help me recognize the hearts in which You want me to plant them. The readiest hearts are not always the obvious ones . . . I know. Thanks for Your wisdom.

Sticks and Stones
USING ETERNAL BUILDING MATERIALS

LIFE LESSON

All of us desire to leave a legacy, to know that we mattered. And our legacy is determined by how we spend our days.

As we've seen, the question becomes, will our influence last beyond our lifetime? Paul was well aware of the correlation between the building materials we use and the quality of the construction. In 1 Corinthians 3:12–14 he wrote, "If any man builds on this foundation [Jesus Christ] using gold, silver, costly stones, wood, hay or straw, his work will be shown for what it is, because the Day will bring it to light. It will be revealed with fire, and the fire will test the quality of each man's work. If what he has built survives, he will receive his reward." Every day we get to choose the materials—either temporary or eternal—we'll build our lives with.

■ Very few things in the universe are eternal. Those that are deserve our full attention and should be the most highly valued aspects of our lives. What ever-enduring entities do your life habits and priorities reflect? Be specific.

1 Chronicles 16:31
Psalm 33:10-11
Psalm 37:18
Psalm 117
Proverbs 10:25
Isaiah 40:6-8
Lamentations 5:19
1 Thessalonians 4:17
1 Peter 1:21-25

A belief is something you hold on to, but a conviction is something that holds you.

Look at the examples of true conviction found in the following passages. What will your life look like when your convictions hold you this strongly?
Matthew 16:21
Acts 14:19-20; 16:20-34
2 Corinthians 8:16-24
Philippians 2:25-30

"For it is in giving that we receive;
It is in pardoning that we are pardoned;
And it is in dying to ourselves
that we are born to eternal life."
                              —St. Augustine

> *God chips away everything in your character that doesn't look like Jesus Christ—*
> *all the character faults and flaws—*
> *because His plan is to perfect you in the*
> *image of His Son.*

▌ Today's Challenge

What life-building materials do you use most often—temporary or eternal? How well will your Life Building stand up after you're gone?

Answer both of these questions prayerfully and honestly. Then choose to address one of them with an action step today. What's one way—even a small way—that you can make sure your legacy leads those who are following you toward God? Or what's one way you can replace temporal building materials with eternal—with your convictions, your character, or your community.

▌ Face Time

Eternal Lord, help me keep my eyes clearly focused on two objects. I never want to lose sight of eternity, of this reality that awaits everyone. And I always want to keep in view the lives of the people I can point in that direction.

Collisions
STAYING THE COURSE WHEN YOUR LIFE CRASHES

LIFE LESSON

Our collisions with God's values and God's will can be remedied when we trust God, delight in God, and commit ourselves to Him.

We get to choose which path we take in life. We can travel in God's direction, or we can chart our own course and try to make it on our own. We can drive the car empowered by His will or the one fueled by our will. When I choose to drive my own car and make all my decisions without consulting Him, it's like heading the wrong way down a one-way street. It ends in a collision with God, which isn't pretty. Only when we allow Him to direct us can we leave a lasting impact. "Trust in the LORD with all your heart and lean not on your own understanding; in all your ways acknowledge him, and he will make your paths straight" (Proverbs 3:5-6).

God longs for us to delight in Him more than we delight in our own freedom. In fact, when we delight in Him, our heart's desires often change. We no longer want our way; we want His way.

■ What happens when we make God our heart's greatest delight?
Deuteronomy 4:29-31
Psalms 42-43
Philippians 1:18-26
Philippians 3:1-14

"It is in recognizing the actual presence of God that we find prayer no longer a chore, but a supreme delight."
—Gordon Lindsay

God says, "You have to commit to following My will, *and* then *I'll* show you what it is."

....

■ Why does God consider it so important that we commit to the Person, not just the plan?
1 Samuel 15:22
Psalm 16:5
Psalm 71:23-26
Psalm 119:57
John 17:3

▶ Today's Challenge

What's one of God's values or one aspect of God's will that you keep bashing into? Do you crash on purpose? Or do you keep forgetting?

Brainstorm one way you might trust God more, one way you might delight in Him more fully, and one way you might commit to Him more wholeheartedly.

Then choose one of these options and make it your goal for today—or for as soon as possible. Bring in a support and accountability partner to help you stay on God's track.

▶ Face Time

Ouch, God! I'm tired of spending time in a spiritual ICU after "encountering" Your unmovable will. You'd think I'd learn.

Well, actually, I think I am learning. I don't want to try this alone anymore. Help me trust You, delight in You, commit myself and my life to You, so I'll recognize You more consistently as my ever-present Companion.

Starfish

MAKING A WORLD OF DIFFERENCE

| LIFE LESSON | *When we recognize the power of one—when we focus on the personal needs of individuals—we'll find ourselves transformed and we'll impact lives for eternity.* |

The problem comes when we start thinking happiness means being safe and comfortable and when our goal in life becomes the avoidance of all risk. When our top priority is to be safe and secure, we lose touch not just with the needs of others but with a primary need of our own. We were created for so much more than punching buttons and scrolling screens. We were created for a grand adventure! God designed us to take great risks and face huge challenges, to accomplish mighty goals that will have a lasting impact.

If you discovered that you only had one month to live and you began considering how you could leave a lasting global legacy, you might be tempted to think, *It's too late. I don't have the money or power needed to make a difference in this world.* But never underestimate the power of one. It's the ability each of us has, every day, to be used by God to bless the rest of the world.

If we make it a habit to do what we can, when we can, where we can, we will be transformed as we help others.

■ Stretch your memory and your imagination. Who are some people, young and old, you encounter often through your week? Think about all the places you go.

■ What might you be able to do for each one of them individually? Think of acts of love that take seconds or minutes, but can change a life.

■ Describe some concrete situations in which God might use you in expected or unexpected ways.
Acts 8:26-39
1 Peter 4:10-11

"As the purse is emptied, the heart is filled."

—*Victor Hugo*

Can you listen and care? offer a smile? hug a child? Most of us underestimate the power we have just by being present in the life of someone else.

■ *According to Jesus (Matthew 25:31-40), what's happening when you "waste" a little time on someone "insignificant"?*

■ *In what specific ways did Jesus model what He taught?*
Luke 8:26-40
Luke 8:41-48
John 3:1-15
John 4

"It is one of the most beautiful compensations of this life that no man can sincerely try to help another without helping himself."

—Ralph Waldo Emerson

▶ Today's Challenge

Choose one.

One man, one woman, or one child whom you know you can bless with a simple, cost-free gift. A smile, a compliment, a door opened, a held elevator.

Choose one. You might make your choice the moment you see the one and act in courteous love. Or you could set your sights on the one now and plan your act of love ahead of time.

From many perspectives, your act of love might seem like a matter of little real impact. From just about any perspective . . . except the perspective belonging to the one.

Go now and create happiness.

▶ Face Time

God, make my heart sensitive to hurting people and help me see others as You see them.

Give me the strength today to see someone's need and meet it in Your strength.

Footprint

LEAVING A LASTING IMPRESSION

LIFE LESSON

We want to be good stewards of our planet because of the responsibility that God has entrusted to us regarding His creation. But while we look for ways to decrease our environmental footprint, we should seek to increase our spiritual footprint. We need to make the most positive, the most lasting imprint on people's lives possible. To do that, we have to get incredibly intentional about the kind of impression we're making on other people's lives.

God loves you just the way you are, but He loves you too much to let you stay that way. See Philippians 2:13.

■ *According to the following passages, in what ways does God's grace manifest itself in both incredible power and infinite love?*
Romans 8:12-14
Romans 13:12-14
1 Peter 2:11-12
2 Peter 1:3-4
Jude 1:24-25

"Treat people as if they were what they ought to be and you help them to become what they are capable of being."
—Johann Wolfgang von Goethe

When we're in the atmosphere of God's grace and feel totally accepted, we crave change. We want to know Him and be more like Him.

■ *What are a few ways God's empowering grace might work in your life?*

John 1:17

Acts 4:33

Acts 6:8

Romans 12:6

1 Corinthians 3:10

1 Corinthians 15:10

2 Corinthians 1:12

▶ Today's Challenge

What do you need in this moment? Do you need a fresh filling of God's forgiving, empowering grace? a dose of grace from another person? the experience of extending grace to someone?

Choose one of those options and make a plan for following through on it as soon as possible—preferably today. Pray about your plan. Consider how it will be a win-win or even a win-win-win—for you, for the other person, and for God.

▶ Face Time

Gracious Father, Your grace is so much more abundant and satisfying than I realized. When You give it to me, I'm getting something that's more valuable than anything earth can offer. And yet it comes from an infinite source—You. There is no end to the supply of grace we're able to receive and exchange.

So help me to be generous but never frivolous in my grace encounters with You and with others.

Game Over
DYING TO LIVE

LIFE LESSON

We were designed to be in perfect relationship with God. We were created with a homesickness for the eternal reality of a place beyond our wildest dreams. As the old hymn explains, "This world is not my home." Heaven is our heart's home, where the homecoming party goes on and on and on. But it's also a place of "no more"—no more tears, grief, loss, or death. "He will wipe every tear from their eyes. There will be no more death or mourning or crying or pain, for the old order of things has passed away" (Revelation 21:4).

> You're not really ready to live until you're ready to die.

■ Restate in your own words a few of the eternity-directed teachings of these passages:
Psalm 27:13-14
Philippians 3:20-21
1 Corinthians 15:12-58
2 Timothy 4:6-8

> "I am a little pencil in the hand of a writing God who is sending a love letter to the world."
>
> —Mother Teresa

What would your daily life look like if you absorbed and completely owned the truths you just read about?

Until you understand the fact that life is preparation for eternity, life won't make sense to you.

■ What is the emotional and spiritual condition of those who deny or ignore eternity?
Ecclesiastes 1:1-11
Matthew 22:23-32
John 18:38

"Find out how much God has given you and from it take what you need; the remainder is needed by others."
—Saint Augustine

■ Even though you say you believe in eternity, if you don't keep it consciously in view and live in light of its reality, what do your actions say you honestly believe?

_____

_____

_____

_____

_____

_____

_____

_____

_____

_____

_____

_____

_____

_____

_____

▶ Today's Challenge

Imagine how different your life would be if you always kept an accurate view of eternity before you. Go ahead. Paint a picture of your hypothetical daily experience in some detail.

Now make it a little less hypothetical. Determine one reachable step you can take in the next hour that will demonstrate your awareness of the end of this life and the forever life that comes after it.

Take that step.

▶ Face Time

Lord, I don't want to die. But I think I'm beginning to want to live even more than I dislike death. Keep drawing me closer to You, closer every day. If I can keep You always before me, then death will become almost like crossing a threshold.

Help me live the next five minutes in a way that will count forever.

I'll check back with You in about five minutes.

Preflight Checklist

❑ I actively watch for chances to touch people's lives.

❑ When I find out what God wants me to do, I usually respond quickly.

❑ I regularly spend time in God's Word.

❑ I strive to consistently focus on actions that have an eternal impact.

❑ Those coming after me on the journey of faith will do well if they follow my example.

❑ Friends could point to at least one godly conviction that drives me.

❑ My enjoyment of God's presence is growing.

❑ I'm getting quicker at yielding to God when I collide with His will.

❑ Others would say that I value individual people and care about their needs.

❑ I regularly invest time, effort, and/or money to help needy people.

❑ I'm usually confident that God's grace is enough for me.

❑ The word *forgive* often comes up in my close relationships.

❑ My awareness of death and eternity has already motivated me to change some priorities.

❑ I make an effort to use words that reflect my focus on eternal rather than temporary matters.

This self-evaluation may help you identify areas for focused development in your life—not necessarily the "most important" areas, but the ones you think God is prompting you to pursue in the coming months. Look back at Days 23 through 29 and choose applications from one or two of your "Live It Up" exercises that you'd like to build into your life. Write them under "Principle 4" in "My Maximum Life Plan" on page 168.

One Month to Live Lifestyle
Bold Ways to Leave

Ready to go? Maybe not. Then let's *get* ready. That will mean different types of preparation for different people. Here are some ideas beyond those we've provided in Days 23 through 29. Look them over and take or adapt the ones that will best help you prepare for the end . . . and for a new beginning.

Parting Passages

Investing in People
2 Corinthians 6:3-10
1 Thessalonians 2:6-9
1 Peter 4:10-11

Eternal Seeds
2 Corinthians 4:16-18
2 Corinthians 5:1
1 Timothy 1:15-16
1 Timothy 6:12

Bridge Building
Exodus 18
Acts 9:26-27; 11:25-26
James 2:14-26
1 Peter 1:6-9

God's Will
Psalm 25:4-13
Psalm 119:1-6
Matthew 16:24-28
Romans 15:4

Preparing
1 Corinthians 15:52-55
1 Timothy 4:7-8
1 Timothy 6:17-19

Quick Takes

Applications requiring a few minutes.

- Forgo a small luxury and use the money to bless someone who needs the encouragement.

- What do you want your eulogy to say about how you've invested your life? Write it down.

- Sit quietly with someone who's hurting.

- Think of someone who might welcome God's salvation message. Brainstorm a few ways to show love and maybe open the door for sharing the good news of Jesus' love.

- Do something good that only God sees.

- Call or e-mail someone who recently made a difference in your life—even a small one—and thank that person.

- Remind yourself of a time when you opposed God's will. What happened?

- Tell God one way He delights you. Or ask Him to help you delight in Him.

- Ask God to change your heart toward someone who bothers you.

Grace
Romans 5:12-21
Ephesians 4:32–5:2
Philippians 4:8-9

The End
Psalm 90
John 3:16-21
2 Corinthians 5:9-10

+ Pray for God's empowering grace to change you in one specific way.

+ Make a small sacrifice for someone you love.

+ Write five questions to ask when you're with God in heaven.

Day Jobs

Applications that take an hour or so.

Pass It On

Gather your children or grandchildren and share one of your life's lessons. Use stories whenever you can.

Be Disturbed

Volunteer at a homeless shelter or some other ministry to those in need. Use the time, not only to meet their needs, but to advance your inner transformation. Ask the people questions. Imagine their lifestyle and self-image. Pray that God would soften your heart's calluses and disturb you because of the physical, emotional, relational, and spiritual needs of these precious people.

Grace for an Hour

Set aside one hour and focus your attention on receiving God's grace and extending His grace to others. During that hour, immediately confess any sin to God and accept His complete grace. Give Him any guilt you feel for sins already forgiven. And determine to extend grace to everyone you encounter. Give those individuals small gifts—smiles, compliments, hugs, a helping hand. Do your best to immediately forgive any small or large offenses. Just love them.

Give to Live

Make a small sacrifice for someone you love such as giving up an activity to spend the time helping him or her. Focus your attention on that person and their enjoyment for the entire time you're with them

Confront Eternity

Hang out in a cemetery and contemplate the certainty of death. But rather than becoming morbid, let this exercise bring focus to your life vision and priorities. Try to get in touch with a sense of urgency regarding your numbered days. Talk to God about His victory over death. Thank Jesus for His incredible sacrifice. During this time, write, record, or illustrate three insights you want to remember or changes you want to make. (Review these once a day for a week.)

Time Release

Applications to be completed over days or weeks.

Vacation from Normalcy

On Day 23, you were challenged to review your calendar, checkbook, and credit card statements to evaluate where you're investing your time and resources. If you haven't done this, do it now. Then choose between two and five possible ways to reallocate your time and money for eternal value.

Now set aside at least three days—or, preferably, an entire week—as a vacation from "life as usual." For just these few days, try out the changes you're considering. Replace a few eternally meaningless investments of time and money with investments that will impact eternity.

Don't try to revolutionize your whole life at once. You might simply exchange some hobby time for family time. Or give up eating out for a week and buy a bag of groceries for an unemployed family. You could shift a half hour a day from magazine reading to Bible or Christian book reading. Or buy a salad instead of a burger and fries.

Journal about your experiences, particularly tracking any eternal fruit you anticipate harvesting because of your wise investments.

Commit to the Person

If you've been waiting to commit until God revealed His plan for your life, you might wait a long time. So commit now. Not to a course of action, but to God Himself.

Devote seven days to pursuing the Person of God. Not to the pursuit of a direction or requests or answers. But to the pursuit of just Him.

For a week, whenever you can, take time to read Bible passages and books about who God is. Sing and listen to songs about Him. Think about and discuss Him with friends and family. Listen to teaching CDs or tapes or radio programs about God.

As you go about your regular activities, surround yourself with reminders of His presence. Smile at Him now and then. Talk to Him about anything at any time, silently or out loud.

When you go to bed, ask Him to fill your dreams. When you wake up, ask Him to fill your day.

Journal about your experience. When the week is over, evaluate the results. Then talk with God about how He wants you to spend the next week.

Game On
LIVING IT UP

LIFE
LESSON

The key to the fulfilled life is passion.

You have been given an extraordinary gift—your life. You have an exceptional calling—to be the very best you God created you to be. Your goal is to unwrap this gift and use all that you've been given in the pursuit of what matters most—loving God and loving other people.

■ As we finish up this month, consider the four key ingredients of passion—love, integrity, forgiveness, and enthusiasm. Why is each of these impossible if we don't stay in constant connection with God?

■ How does each of these enhance and enrich our connection with God?

■ What are you willing to invest in order to maximize these four ingredients of passion to maximize your life?

"You can't lead anyone else further
than you have gone yourself."
—Gene Mauch

How do you feel knowing that Jesus has already fulfilled the mission you're on—the mission to live passionately, love completely, learn humbly, and leave boldly?

"If a man would move the world, he must first move himself."

—Socrates

Now it's time for you to pull together the fruit of your month's journaling, prayer, and adventurous living—and plan to let the month continue. Indefinitely.

Turn to "My Maximum Life Plan" and consider our challenge to continue the One Month to Live lifestyle. The application goals you've collected in the "Plan" are the cream-of-the-crop life changes you want to make. Add, subtract, or edit as God and you see fit. Just continue taking passionate steps into life, steps toward God Himself.

"Life is short and we have never too much time for gladdening the hearts of those who are traveling the dark journey with us. Oh be swift to love, make haste to be kind."

—Henri Frédéric Amiel

▶ Face Time

Please keep me from forgetting the insights or relaxing the convictions I've gained this month. Make me strong and truly committed to the small steps of spiritual health and growth that will only build my passion and understanding.

I don't ever want to be less in love with You than I am now. In fact, I only want more. And more.

_____

_____

_____

_____

_____

_____

_____

_____

_____

_____

_____

_____

When your thirty-day commitment to this adventure is finished, what then? Your month is up . . .

Now we challenge you to become a lifer.

Here's where you can map out the One Month to Live lifestyle for the next month. And the next year. Until the moment of your last breath. Plan intentionally to evict regret from your future. Set yourself up for *maximum life!*

We've prompted you at the end of each week—four times in this book—to choose one or two applications from your "Live It Up" exercises and write them here. Now review the goals you've collected, talk to God about His plan for your next month, and narrow down your options to at least two and no more than four goals to pursue over the next thirty days. You can either highlight them or write them under "My Next Month to Live."

Take time to think through the details. Do you need to plan specific, individual steps? When and where will you work to carry out your goals? Whom will you involve as active participants or as prayer and accountability partners? How will you know when you've achieved your goals?

We also encourage you to photocopy this plan and share it with your prayer and accountability partners.

And now . . . to life!

My Maximum Life Plan

Principle 1:

Live Passionately

Application goals from Days 2–8 to build into my life over the next month:

Principle 2:
Love Completely

Application goals from Days 9–15 to build into my life over the next month:

Principle 3:
Learn Humbly

Application goals from Days 16–22 to build into my life over the next month:

Principle 4:
Leave Boldly

Application goals from Days 23–30 to build into my life over the next month:

My Next Month to Live

Two, three, or four application goals for the next thirty days:

Journaling